The Relational Origins
of Prejudice

The Library of Object Relations
Series Editors:
David E. Scharff and Jill Savege Scharff

The Library of Object Relations provides an expanding body of theory for understanding individual development and pathology, human interaction, and new avenues of treatment. They apply to realms of experience from the internal world of the individual to the human community, from the clinical situation to everyday life, and from individual psychoanalysis and psychotherapy, to group therapy, couple and family therapy, and to social policy.

New and featured titles in the series:

The Relational Origins of Prejudice

A Convergence of Psychoanalytic and Social Cognitive Perspectives

RON B. AVIRAM

JASON ARONSON

Lanham • Boulder • New York • Toronto • Plymouth, UK

Published in the United States of America
by Jason Aronson
An imprint of Rowman & Littlefield Publishers, Inc.

A wholly owned subsidiary of
The Rowman & Littlefield Publishing Group, Inc.
4501 Forbes Boulevard, Suite 200, Lanham, Maryland 20706
www.rowmanlittlefield.com

Estover Road
Plymouth PL6 7PY
United Kingdom

British Library Cataloguing in Publication Information Available

Library of Congress Cataloging-in-Publication Data

Aviram, Ron B., 1962-
  The relational origins of prejudice : a convergence of psychoanalytic and social
cognitive perspectives / Ron B. Aviram.
      p. cm. — (The library of object relations)
    Includes bibliographical references.
    ISBN-13: 978-0-7657-0506-8 (cloth : alk. paper)
    ISBN-10: 0-7657-0506-0 (cloth : alk. paper)
    ISBN-13: 978-0-7657-0629-4 (electronic)
    ISBN-10: 0-7657-0629-6 (electronic)
  1. Prejudices. 2. Psychoanalysis. 3. Social perception. I. Title.
  BF575.P9A95 2009
  303.3'85—dc22   2008036668

Printed in the United States of America

⊗™ The paper used in this publication meets the minimum requirements of American
National Standard for Information Sciences—Permanence of Paper for Printed Library
Materials, ANSI/NISO Z39.48-1992.

For My Parents
Ari and Penina

Contents

Acknowledgments

Several people influenced the completion of this book in important ways. I am grateful to them for offering their time, thoughtfulness, and support. In particular, Sandra Buechler helped me find as much clarity as possible in countless discussions about the subject. Also, David Scharff encouraged this project from the beginning and read the entire manuscript and provided very important feedback. Also, I very much appreciate the generosity of friends and colleagues who took the time to read parts, or all, of the manuscript and offered their comments and suggestions. They include: Christopher Bonovitz, Elissa Ganz, Jose Genua, and Elizabeth Hirky. I want to acknowledge my family and friends for their constant presence in my life, which made it possible to write: in particular, my parents, also, Nathy, Andrea, Satchel, Sawyer, and Scarlet Aviram, Rina Aviram, Colin Studds, Andy Burger, Jon Fox, and Randy Kessler. I want to thank Anny Castillo, who was always reliable and cheerful as the research assistant on this project. I am grateful to Art Pomponio, Julie Kirsch, Jessica Bradfield, and Michael Wiles at Rowman and Littlefield.

Chapter One

Introduction

The current Presidential election in the United States highlights how difficult it is to avoid categorizing people according to large group affiliations. The three main contenders for the Presidential election were ascribed membership to a large group based on external features. The automatic categorization to race, gender, and age is unavoidable even though the categories may not be meaningful to the candidates themselves. Furthermore, each of the categories overlaps with the others within each individual. Still, the media speculated whether prejudices about any one of these categorical aspects of the candidates would be a factor in the election. The country seemed to be divided into constituencies that were identified according to race, gender, age group, religion, ethnicity, class, and so on. People had to ask themselves to what extent prejudice affects their choices or the choices of their neighbors. The prejudices being confronted were racism, sexism, ageism, and possibly prejudice against Moslems and Mormons, liberals and conservatives, immigrants and class differences. Yet the questions posed about prejudice were unclear. Would people cast their votes based on a prejudice against women, or African Americans, or older adults? That suggests a prejudice akin to hatred. Or, would people vote in support of the person who looked most like themselves or believed in the same values? Is that kind of favoritism a prejudice, and if so is it associated with a prejudice of hatred? The context forces people to notice large group categorizations. Even if they do not regularly think in terms of large group affiliations, people notice if they are alike or not with others in terms of large group memberships. The interrelationship of the individual and the large group is central in our effort to understand the underlying motivations of prejudice.

Each large group category along with the potential accompanying prejudice is related to an important aspect of identity. The example of the election shows how identity can become salient when others impose a category membership onto a person. It forces any individual to acknowledge aspects of himself or herself that are perceived by others to be part of his or her identity. This has the potential to impact the way people feel about themselves and may affect how they are treated by others. Individuals are also active in developing large group identity as a vital aspect of self. When a large group category is emotionally meaningful, it is part of a self-system, and, when salient, it affects perceptions and feelings.

A book about prejudice is fundamentally about identity, and therefore it is interrelated with our need to answer the question, "who am I?" This basic question organizes our environment as well as our internal experience of ourselves. Knowing who I am pertains to the question, "who else is like me?" At the macrosocial level this is known as the ingroup. Usually this ingroup is part of our identity, a dimension of the self-concept that social psychologists call collective identity. The instant an ingroup is formulated in the mind we become aware of who belongs to the ingroup and all others who do not. Those who do not belong to the ingroup make up the outgroup. These are the basic components upon which prejudice plays out in human relations. In simplest terms, the prejudice differentiates between two identity groups: an ingroup and an outgroup. The perspective that will be developed in this book is that prejudice is a result of an aberration in the relationship of the individual with his or her ingroup. The internal and external experience of the person associated with the developmental and contextual conditions that affect this process will be the focus of the following chapters.

Because prejudice is a longstanding human behavior, we can speculate that it has a purpose. Based on processes of evolution that favored conditions that promoted survivability, the brain process that categorizes was basic for the capacity of people to organize into groups. This tends to be a necessary condition of safety for many mammals (Bowlby, 1969). Given that mankind has developed as a potential predator upon its own kind, the groupings that were organized were to protect not only from animal predators, but also from other human groups. So much of human history reflects a struggle between human groups, that we can wonder whether it is an inevitable aspect of the human condition. If we concede that the problem of prejudice manifests in and between societies when individuals perceive themselves and others as large group members, then we must examine the conditions that facilitate collective or large group identity as a way to potentially understand what is occurring.

The focus on identity formation directs attention to developmental precursors that begin with the interaction of the infant and caregiver and ultimately influence how the adult interacts with the large groups of his or her environ-ment. The early phase of development in which the infant depends upon the caregiver for safety, as well as a beginning sense of self, is paralleled later in development when the individual interacts with large groups. At both stages this interrelationship is unavoidable and inevitable. Our capacity to attend to processes of separation and attachment is central to understanding these in-teractions. The young child struggles to manage security in terms of auton-omy as an individual, while remaining attached to the caregiver. Similarly, the young adult manages autonomy as an individual while developing an attach-ment and sense of belonging with the large group. At both stages we can con-ceive of an optimal balance between separation and attachment needs.

RELATIONAL PERSPECTIVE AND THE LARGE GROUP

A relational perspective has become central in psychoanalysis. The conscious and unconscious motivations of a relational theory of human behavior are geared toward facilitating secure, safe, and cooperative relationships with im-portant individuals, from the initial caregivers to peers and intimate partners. Psychoanalysis offers a clinical method to address the irrational and destruc-tive behavior that people engage in with each other. So far it has focused on interpersonal dynamics, and therefore has been unable to say much about the influence of large groups upon individuals. This was in large part responsible for the abandonment of psychoanalytic theory in the effort to address preju-dice in the second half of the twentieth century.

By incorporating the large group as a potential object with which individ-uals establish an important relationship, it is possible to extend the parame-ters of psychoanalysis. A relational theory of prejudice sheds light on the po-tential convergence of ideas from psychoanalysis and social psychology. Psychoanalytic theories are primarily concerned with interpersonal relation-ships and unconscious processes that manifest in maladaptive interpersonal choices, or subjective states of vulnerability, and so on; however, psychoana-lytic theories of prejudice do not discuss the ingroup and outgroup. This lim-its psychoanalytic efforts to address prejudice because models of interper-sonal dynamics are applied to a large group phenomenon. The two levels of experience may have some similarities but are not identical, and they have different operating principles in important ways. On the other hand, social psychological efforts to address prejudice are primarily focused on the inter-action of the individual and the large group. Studies of social cognitive psy-chology are interested in understanding how large groups influence people, and to some extent individual differences, but there is less attention to the way large groups might interact with intrapsychic experience, or how psychopathology may interact with the large group.

THE LARGE GROUP IN THE MIND

W. R. D. Fairbairn (1952) elaborated a model of interpersonal relations that prioritized the relational nature of people. Given this starting point, he was able to define pathology as a process that impedes satisfying and cooperative relationships. His theory of mind included a way to understand how aspects of interactions with caregivers remain unconscious throughout development and affect the quality of interpersonal relations later in life. Some of Fairbairn's writing refers to societal structures, but he does not elaborate on a way to understand how one's relationship to the large group can be represented in the mind. His writing left us to determine whether the relationship between an individual and large group is in any way different from identifications with historical interpersonal relationships. This is an area that will be further developed and clarified in chapter 4.

Importantly, social psychological studies find that people can be influenced by large groups in different ways than they are by the interpersonal relationships in their lives. If this is a meaningful distinction, then the point reached in Fairbairn's theorizing does not account for the independent influence of large groups. The description of object relations that Fairbairn elaborated would lead to the formulation that large groups can be integrated into the mind as parental substitutes, and therefore the large group does not need to be attended to directly. From a clinical perspective, this would imply that by addressing the interpersonal context one is also addressing any large group issues. This was the best that could be formulated in Fairbairn's lifetime, but today we can integrate evidence from social cognitive psychology about the independent function of the large group in the mind. We could also elaborate additional ways to discuss the intrapsychic implications of collective identity, and in particular how these identifications are associated with prejudice.

By providing a conceptual scheme for the large group in the mind, we are able to account for conditions in which people behave in ways that are unexpected given their interpersonal histories. Object relationships traditionally are about the relationship with one other significant person. By conceptually offering a place in the mind for the large group, we are better able to speak about the relationship of the individual in the large group. I have called this object relationship a *social object* representation to provide a place for the large group in the mind. In essence the social object is the representation of the identification with the large group. This large group representation would have to be interrelated with object representations of interpersonal relationships because they precede the individual's relationship to the large group. Yet, the large group in a person's life does have an independent impact on experiences of security and threat, self-esteem, and modes of interaction in the world.

For example, individuals who belong to a stigmatized large group may be affected by this membership in ways that are unrelated to the quality of the person's interpersonal history. This is especially relevant given that most societies are structured in hierarchical power relations between large groups (Dalal, 2002; Duckitt, 1992). Interpersonal relationships may develop in satisfying or unsatisfying ways that can change when functioning within the large groups. Another example could be a young woman who grew up in an abusive or neglectful environment. She may experience little support from her family, and opportunities to advance in her life may appear limited. This young person could find acceptance and a sense of belonging by joining a gang (or army, cult, religious organization, etc.). The strength of the social object will depend on the degree of vulnerability or threat she experiences. Threat can be developmentally shaped, or it can be environmentally present. The social object will have greater influence if the threat to her security is strong. In her case, relationships with fellow gang members may be rewarding, and self-esteem could be enhanced as she advances within the gang. The gang is a compensation for some vulnerability and helps ward off other psychological difficulties. Belonging to one gang automatically places the person in contrast to other gangs and may make one hypervigilant, needing to be aware of rival gang members in the environment. In a context that highlights the large group, we can say that collective identity is salient. In other words, it is conscious. When collective identity is salient, people think of themselves and others as large group members, and perceptions of self and other reflect ingroup and outgroup status.

PREJUDICE AND THE INDIVIDUAL

Processes of separation and attachment influence the potential of affiliation throughout development. Initially this is oriented toward the caregiver, but as development proceeds it involves interpersonal relations and, ultimately, the relationship the individual has with large groups. Healthy development is dependent upon an optimal balance between separation and attachment processes. Prejudice occurs when there is a loss of optimal balance in the capacity to be an autonomous individual while experiencing belonging to the large group.

The problem of prejudice can be understood to be a result of an *overidentification* between an individual and a large group. An overidentification eliminates the boundary between the individual and the large group. This is simultaneously associated with psychological defenses that eliminate the complexity of the environment such that ingroup and outgroup members are perceived as homogeneous. Defenses of splitting, rationalization, and denial are central to prejudice. The overidentification may be an outcome of developmental deficits or an environmental context that highlights large group conditions.

Fairbairn's model accounts for a pathology that blurs the boundary between the individual and large group in terms of primary identification. Pathology in individuals, according to Fairbairn, results from interpersonal experiences that do not facilitate what he called a mature dependence, leaving the infant and growing child to experience an infantile dependence with the caregiver. Fairbairn believes that dependence is lifelong and unavoidable. His theory implies that the degrees of dependence progress from lack of differentiation (primary identification) to mature dependence, which offers both more autonomy and connection. We know that young children can distinguish between ingroups and outgroups, and in adolescence the young person establishes relationships with large groups in the society in the course of identity formation. If primary identification continues and affects interpersonal relationships in adulthood, then we can presume that an overidentification with the large group is also possible. This would be a prototype of the prejudiced person who uses the large group as a compensation for the underlying vulnerability of infantile dependence. We can suggest that the individual who uses the large group as a compensation will be prejudiced regardless of environmental conditions that emphasize more or less salience of the large group. For this person the large group is always salient because there is no differentiation between the large group and the self.

This experience was put into words by the protagonist general in the film *Letters from Iwo Jima*. In a scene in which he is asked, "How would you feel if America and Japan were to enter the war?" he responds, "If this were to happen, I would have to serve my duty to my country. . . . I'd have to follow my convictions." Someone asks him, "Do you mean you'd have to follow your convictions or your country's convictions?" and he replies, "Are they not the same?" This is an example of the potential of a context to eliminate the boundary between the individual and the large group. War often does this on a massive scale. The prejudiced person who maintains prejudices regardless of context can be understood to have a pathology that Fairbairn would describe as one form of continuation of infantile dependence and is characterized by a primary identification with important people or groups. This intrapsychic model requires the addition of a social object representation to provide a place in the mind for the large group.

In the following chapters I will describe a model that seeks convergence between a relational psychoanalysis and social cognitive psychology. In the past fifty years the two disciplines have separated their efforts to address prejudice. One approach is primarily interpersonal and values the intrapsychic space that both is shaped by and affects the environment. The other approach recognizes that individuals always function within groups, both physically and psychologically. Yet the psychological implications of development that can impact how the individual responds to the environment is de-emphasized. Obviously the effort to combine the two perspectives may be able to enhance the overall effort. Erikson (1959) states that a psychosocial developmental theory would need to develop to fully appreciate the implications of identity. Given the relevance of identity to the study of prejudice, it is vital to seek conceptual schemes that converge across multiple disciplines.

This book introduces the compatibility between relational psychoanalysis and social cognitive psychology in the effort to address the problem of prejudice. A relational perspective in psychoanalysis and social cognitive psychology highlights that considerable overlap already exists between the two disciplines. In many ways, attention to this problem requires the knowledge of both disciplines in that prejudice is an outcome of developmental factors, intrapsychic process, interpersonal functioning, and societal conditions. The individual engages in prejudice at the point at which he or she comes into contact with society, and therefore prejudice is also dependent upon identity formation. The developmental precursors of identity formation and the contextual conditions that influence identity should not be studied separately, but rather they should be intertwined in a broadened effort to address the problem.

The chapters that follow can be read on their own; however, as a whole the chapters build upon each other, and conceptually, I hope, each enhances the previous to provide an overall model that engages the interdependence of both psychoanalytic and social cognitive perspectives.

Chapter 2 provides an overview of the major theories of prejudice from the psychoanalytic and social psychological literatures. It will become clear how the development of the psychological study on prejudice began as a common effort across disciplines only to diverge in the latter half of the twentieth century. The development of the relational perspective in psychoanalysis offers a bridge with social psychology that can converge and potentially integrate knowledge from the two fields in order to further our effort to address prejudice.

In chapter 3 the foundation for a relational conceptualization of prejudice will be developed. A re-definition of prejudice will clarify the relational implications for understanding this problem along with the developmental precursors of identity formation. The potential to integrate diverse literatures will become apparent in this chapter, bringing together broad discussions about separation and attachment processes, which will be shown to be central to managing identity and prejudice.

In chapter 4 a detailed discussion of object relations theory of prejudice is presented. Fairbairn's theory is brought into focus because he offers an intrapsychic model that is not readily available in a general psychoanalytic relational theory. Furthermore, Fairbairn's emphasis on dependence as a lifelong process is congruent with a social psychological perspective on the lifelong dependence on groups that individuals cannot avoid. An object relations model of large groups is presented that expands the range of inquiry for psychoanalysis and introduces the social object representation.

Chapter 5 presents an integration of attachment theory offered by Bowlby and Ainsworth, with the recent work in social psychology on attachment theory in romantic relationships and in relation to large group affiliations. Attachment theory is an important perspective to integrate into the discussion about prejudice because of the strong use of evolution theory. The underlying emphasis on survival is an important variable to consider when discussing the relationship of the individual and the large group. The relevance of threat is part of this perspective that helps explain the intensity of prejudice.

Chapter 6 follows up on the role of threat in prejudice. Individuals can experience both internal and external threat that is psychologically experienced as annihilation anxiety. This helps account for the extreme behavior encountered with prejudice. This chapter discusses the way that large groups may be part of the psychoanalytic process even if it is not acknowledged. The large group in the consulting room suggests that clinicians can attend to the societal dimension in the person by attending to collective identity. This is an area that is just beginning to acquire a language and conceptual relevance to clinical work.

Chapter 7 pulls it all together by offering a synthesis of the relational origins of prejudice. This chapter organizes the material discussed in the other chapters to provide a coherent overview of the interrelationship of psychoanalytic and social psychological perspectives. Although psychoanalysis is a discipline that works with people, usually one at a time, to repair pathology of interpersonal relations, the broader society is always part of the process. Similarly, although social psychological approaches tend to address normal processes that impact all individuals, the unconscious mind and the pathology of individuals should not be excluded. The most recent work on multiple identities in social psychology offers another potential to converge with the growing understanding of self-states. It will include an examination of the role of aggression in prejudice.

A century enriched by theories and diverse research about the psychology of prejudice has passed. Knowledge acquired from different disciplines in psychology can be integrated to form a coherent model that attends to multiple levels of experience simultaneously. Overlapping conceptual schemes in psychoanalysis and social psychology can orient the focus of inquiry about prejudice by using our knowledge of the experience of the large group within the individual.

Chapter Two

Major Theories of Prejudice

The effort to understand the etiology and dynamics of prejudice has been pursued by both psychoanalysts and social psychologists as each field progressed in the last century. Initially, the unique perspective each field brought to the study was complementary; however, the differences in emphasis and lack of progress eventually led to abandoning the prospects of a synthesis of ideas. Today the contributions of both disciplines seem to converge in a general relational orientation. This offers an opportunity to integrate two levels of analysis that together reveal a dialectical engagement between the intrapsychic and macrosocial human experience. This chapter highlights the major contributions from psychoanalysis and social psychology in the last century. Examining these contributions side by side draws attention to the significant overlapping possibilities and that the evolution of ideas in both disciplines has developed to a point which is newly available for integration.

PSYCHOANALYSIS AND THE GROUP

The founder of psychoanalysis, Sigmund Freud, lived during a time when individual prejudices associated with collective identities converged with societal conditions that unleashed the destructive consequences of nationalistic fervor during the First World War, and the hatred and aggression of prejudice as National Socialism emerged in Germany following that war. He was clearly aware that the acceptability of psychoanalysis in Europe could be limited because he was a Jew. This was one factor that influenced his support of Carl Jung to become his successor, over several others in his inner circle who happened to be Jewish. A subtle, but very important implication of this example recognizes that Freud's Jewishness became important in that context, regardless of his personal association with Judaism. In other words, this aspect of his collective identity was ascribed by others onto Freud, and it affected his choices and behavior. Freud personally did not possess religious faith or a strong ethnic identification (Freud, 1926), yet this example is indicative of how group identity can be affected by external conditions. It indicates how identity not only may be internally generated and meaningful, but can also be externally imposed with all the potential implications and consequences associated with prejudice that influence perception and behavior.

There is very little direct reference in Freud's writing about prejudice. This is not an indication of his lack of awareness or concern about intergroup dynamics. Consider the following comment he made reflecting collective identity and prejudice in society that was directed at his ingroup. In his autobiographical study, Freud (1935/1963) writes, "I found that I was expected to feel myself inferior and an alien because I was a Jew. I refused absolutely to do the first of these things. I have never been able to see why I should feel ashamed of my descent or, as people were beginning to say, of my race. I put up, without much regret, with my nonacceptance into the community" (p. 14). His comment hints at two fundamental potential reactions that individuals may experience during intergroup contact. It is apparent from Freud's remark that individuals may become defiant or, in contrast, experience shame about the devaluing attitude that is imposed upon them by the surrounding community.

Freud's major statement about the relationship between the individual and the large group is written in his monograph, *Group Psychology and the Analysis of the Ego* (1921). His emphasis was on the relationship of unconscious identifications that occur between individuals and have implications for group formation. This is depicted as a process of identification among group members that facilitates a mutual replacement of an ego ideal with a leader.

In this monograph, Freud (1921) makes his most direct statements pertaining to intergroup prejudice. He draws an analogy to the emotional relations that evolve between two people who are intimately involved with each other. In all such relationships, Freud believes, feelings of aversion and hostility are also present. Most of the time these negative emotions are repressed and out of awareness. For our purposes, this pertains to the likelihood that prejudices can be unconscious in many people. Freud continues,

> The same thing happens when men come together in larger units. Every time two families become connected by a marriage, each of them thinks itself superior to or of better birth than the other. Of two neighboring towns each is the other's most jealous rival; every little canton looks down upon the others with contempt. Closely related races keep one another at arm's length; the South German cannot endure the North German, the Englishman casts every kind of aspersion upon the Scot, the Spaniard despises the Portuguese. We are no longer astonished that greater differences should lead to an almost insuperable repug-

nance, such as the Gallic people feel for the German, the Aryan for the Semite, and the white races for the colored. (p. 33)

Freud explains this intergroup hostility in terms of narcissism, or self-love. This was an important comment that was subsequently not well developed in psychoanalytic writing on prejudice; however, this is a forerunner to the parallel conceptual work on ingroup favoritism that emerged in the social psychological literature. I will return to this concept shortly. Still, regardless of the apparent truth of the antipathies that Freud referred to, it does not help us to understand why such animosities between large groups or individuals with profound prejudices manifest.

It is striking in reading Freud how much he not only anticipated but also accepted that he could not answer at that time. In the *Group Psychology* monograph, he comments on the two major themes that ultimately became the focus for the social psychological and psychoanalytic study of prejudice. The first theme, which actually took longer before it was studied, is expressed in the following comment. Freud (1921) writes, "there do exist other mechanisms for emotional ties [in addition to self-love], the so-called identifications, insufficiently-known processes and hard to describe, the investigation of which will for some time keep us away from the subject of group psychology" (p. 36). It took about forty more years before social psychologists began to focus specifically on the role of identification processes in the experience of group belongingness and intergroup relations. This comment also points us in the direction that this book will further elaborate, regarding identification processes within individuals, between individuals, and between the individual and the large group, while seeking areas of convergence between psychoanalytic and social psychological efforts.

The second theme focuses on the problem from an individual differences perspective. It involves the internal mechanisms that are associated with prejudice. Freud writes, "it is unmistakable that in this whole connection men give evidence of a readiness for hatred, an aggressiveness, *the source of which is unknown and to which one is tempted to ascribe an elementary character*" (Freud, 1921, p. 34; emphasis added). The relationship between character and prejudice became the first focus of subsequent psychoanalytic theory and research immediately following the Second World War. One of the major efforts that took that approach was the project on the authoritarian personality.

THE AUTHORITARIAN PERSONALITY

Following the Second World War questions about the potential aberrant interrelationship between an individual and the large group became paramount

in an effort to understand how people in any society could take part in geno-
cide. Obviously this question remains with us today. At that time, in the
United States, a research group in Berkeley sought to explain this in terms of
individual character. Their psychoanalytic premise ultimately minimized
Freudian libido theory, and preferred to elaborate significant psychodynamics and defenses that may be identifiable and reflective of a characterological
type, a type of person that they called the authoritarian personality (Adorno,
Frenkel-Brunswik, Levinson, & Sanford, 1950).

There was an enthusiastic response to the explanatory potential of the authoritarian personality. Their effort included both psychoanalytic and sociological processes. Following the war it must have seemed crucial to try to find
an explanation for the atrocities of Nazi ideology and Japanese militarism. To
suggest that prejudiced attitudes and behavior can be identifiable in certain
personality types would have been relieving. However, as Hanna Arendt exposed in her book, *Eichmann in Jerusalem* (1963), people like the Nazi bu-
reaucrat Eichmann may be more similar to ourselves than is comfortable.

In the decades following the publication of the authoritarian personality, researchers began to focus on one particular scale that was developed to measure the prejudiced personality. The F-scale, short for fascist, became a focal
point of considerable controversy regarding the validity of this instrument for
identifying prejudiced individuals. The emphasis of the scale was on the underlying psychodynamics of the potential fascist, and moved away from other
significant aspects of the research project, specifically the relevance of ingroups and outgroups for individuals with prejudiced attitudes. Unfortunately, much of the research that ensued primarily used the F-scale to single
out and classify authoritarian personality as the prejudiced person in society.
Significant criticisms about the inadequacy of the psychometric properties of
the scale led to the ultimate abandonment of much of this research (Altemeyer, 1981).

Not surprisingly, however, one of the initial studies in the authoritarian personality project did emphasize intergroup relations, though this became a secondary consideration for these researchers, as well as many following them.
The study of ethnocentric ideology attempted to measure beliefs regarding
specific large groups, the generality of outgroup rejection, content of ideas
about ingroups and outgroups, and stereotypes about large groups in general.
Given their sociopsychological perspective, the Berkeley group clarifies that
perceptions of ingroups and outgroups reflect identifications and associated
contraidentifications. These psychological reactions imply significantly more
than simply indicating formal membership in a large group. For example,
they elaborate that an outgroup must involve a "basic conflict, of mutual ex-
clusiveness, of violation of primary values" (p. 147), which is experienced as

a contraidentification by the ingroup member. In other words outgroups and their members are incompatible with the ingroup. They conclude that, "ethnocentrism is based on a pervasive and rigid ingroup-outgroup distinction; it involves stereotyped negative imagery and hostile attitudes regarding outgroups, stereotyped positive imagery and submissive attitudes regarding ingroups, and a hierarchical authoritarian view of group interaction in which ingroups are rightly dominant, outgroups subordinate" (p. 150). They further clarify that the content of ethnocentric ideology views outgroups as weaker, but threatening in their desire to gain power. An ethnocentrist worldview perceives this as a permanent and irresolvable state that initiates a hierarchy in which the "superior" ingroup must remain dominant over the "subordinate" outgroup. The ethnocentrist experiences the world in terms of group belonging, and individuals are always perceived as ingroup or outgroup members.

The important question here is why do ethnocentrists maintain this ingroup-outgroup orientation? One answer involves the dynamics of identification, to which these authors alluded; however, they abandoned this as a key element to understanding prejudice. These authors saw that the individual with an ethnocentric orientation needs outgroups to compensate for a weakness in the self, and so is unable to form what Erikson (1985) would call a superordinate identification with humanity as a whole. By not emphasizing the role of identification, I think, they missed an important opportunity to place the data they were gathering into an appropriate framework that makes an association between developmental processes, large group identifications, and prejudice. If they would have pursued this line of inquiry further, the way large groups are represented in the mind and emotional world of individuals would become the basis of intergroup hostility and prejudice. As mentioned in the previous chapter, identity is important for individual-level functioning, but it also has simultaneous implications for intergroup relations. Identification processes appear to be informative about individual-level normal affiliations with large groups and aberrations in this process, and it also suggests how societal conditions can affect a majority of people in a community to experience increased or decreased ingroup identification. Attending to identification processes becomes relevant on an individual level and the intergroup-process level simultaneously. The emphasis can be on one person, or a group of people, and would help us to understand how a common, perhaps ubiquitous, process of ingroup favoritism could cross over to become outgroup aggression.

Adorno and his coauthors (1950), in the effort to identify and minimize an ethnocentrist perspective, and thereby prejudice, write that it is necessary to eliminate "the stereotypical ingroup-outgroup distinction and all that goes with it" (p. 148). I do not think that is possible. In fact, identification, first with parents and family, and later with larger societal groups, is necessary and unavoidable. The effort to understand the dynamics associated with processes of identification and the emotional function that identification serves for the security of the individual, I believe, is central to understanding prejudice. For interpersonal relations and the affiliations of individuals with large groups, the continuum from underidentification to overidentification has important implications. In chapter 4 I will describe how object relations theory can help us understand this dynamic in more depth. The field of social psychology took another two decades before a renewed emphasis on the relevance of large group identifications emerged. This program was developed by Henri Tajfel in his social identity theory, which will be discussed shortly.

Before proceeding to more recent developments, keep in mind that the researchers of the authoritarian personality did elaborate many relevant psychodynamic features of potentially prejudiced individuals that should not be overlooked. For example, during interviews about family relations, prejudiced subjects tended to idealize their parents. In other words, they emphasized the superiority of the family. This stemmed from a basic insecurity about autonomy and an underlying need for parental care, perhaps understood in terms of the parents' authority. The psychodynamic formulation of an authoritarian personality suggests that this type of person had punitive parenting, which leads to hostility toward authority. However, hostility is repressed because the child is dependent upon these authority figures, and thereby it is displaced toward a weaker target. This kind of psychodynamic formulation is mildly satisfying and could be valid in some cases, but it is short of accounting for the general prevalence of prejudice in society, the emotional intensity of prejudice, or the contextually bound expression of prejudice. Importantly, from my perspective, it disregards the relevance of the large group in the mind in favor of an intrapsychic process that is too bound to interpersonal relations of historic significance.

Daniel Levinson, the author of the chapters on ethnocentrism, defines ethnocentrism as an ideology that concerns ingroups and outgroups and their interaction. I agree with Levinson's intended focus on ingroups and outgroups, and although I will take a different approach to understanding the intrapsychic and developmental implications for the individual in relation to large group affiliations, much of the same information and dynamics that I am interested in were identified then. Unfortunately, following publication of the authoritarian personality, psychoanalysts did not continue to develop a coherent line of research and theory about prejudice. The basic psychoanalytic theory of prejudice that was elaborated in this work seemed to be passed down across the generations without much further thought or new developments. In contrast, rather than blindly accepting the theory, following a period of inconclusive research, most social psychologists dismissed this work altogether.

ERICH FROMM AND AUTHORITARIANISM

Erich Fromm was a colleague of Adorno, and part of the Frankfurt school, which emphasized a Marxist sociological perspective. He did not directly participate in the authoritarian personality project in Berkeley; however, more than a decade earlier Fromm elaborated a highly detailed account of authoritarianism in his book, *Escape From Freedom* (1941/1963). As described by Fromm, the person with an authoritarian character will "give up independence of one's individual self and fuse one's self with somebody or something outside of oneself in order to acquire the strength which the individual self is lacking" (p. 141). Fromm states that this sort of symbiotic compensation is an effort to avoid the intolerable aloneness of the individual self. The vulnerability of the authoritarian character could be further understood in Fromm's comments about identity. In *The Sane Society* (1955/1966) Fromm describes how identity is vital for human sanity. He acknowledges that Western culture is directed toward the experience of individuality. However, for the majority, individualism is really a facade covering up the failure to acquire "an individual sense of identity." Fromm writes, "Many substitutes for a truly individual sense of identity were sought for, and found. Nation, religion, class, and occupation serve to furnish a sense of identity" (p. 63), and

> the need to feel a sense of identity stems from the very condition of human existence, and it is a source of the most intense strivings. Since I cannot remain sane without a sense of 'I,' I am driven to do almost anything to acquire this sense. Behind the intense passion for status and conformity is this very need, and it is sometimes even stronger than the need for physical survival. What could be more obvious than the fact that people are willing to risk their lives, to give up their love, to surrender their freedom, to sacrifice their own thoughts, for the sake of being one of the herd, of conforming, and thus acquiring a sense of identity, even though it is an illusory one (p. 64)

Interestingly, what Fromm calls "substitutes of identity" became the central focus of the social cognitive approach to the study of intergroup processes. Obviously, an empirical science needs measurable criteria, and the cognitively knowable elements of identity that Fromm points to can and do help people experience one dimension of identity, collective identity. It is relevant to consider why it is that so much hostility and tension in the world play out through these aspects of identity. Perhaps they are a cover for some deficiency, as

Fromm suggests. Fonagy and Higgitt's (2007) association of prejudice with ontology does put these comments into perspective. The ontological problem that prejudice represents seems to join the analytic emphasis on the self with the social psychological emphasis on the large group. It is precisely when these elements of identity merge, in other words, when the self and the large group become identical, that it does become an ontological problem of Being, and survival of one depends on the survival of the other. This fits with Fromm's comments about the extremes to which people are willing, or needing, to go to in order to acquire, or rather hold onto, a sense of identity (Being).

OPTIMAL DISTINCTIVENESS THEORY

The social psychological parallel to Fromm's elaboration of deindividuation in authoritarianism was provided by Marilyn Brewer (1991) in her Optimal Distinctiveness Theory. While Fromm's theory is strictly about individual functioning with an emphasis on autonomy, Brewer's theory never loses sight of the continuous influence of the group in the mind and emotional world of the individual. Brewer's (1991) work is important to understanding part of the experience of individuals who may be overly dependent upon their group affiliation for self-esteem. She proposes to explain individual functioning in a group context. She believes that "social identity [collective identity] is derived from a fundamental tension between human needs for validation and similarity to others, on one hand, and a countervailing need for uniqueness and individuation, on the other" (1991, p. 477). In her view, collective identity requires a compromise between "differentiation" and "assimilation" from others as group members. The optimal distinctiveness model suggests that an extreme along the inclusiveness dimension (of either differentiation or assimilation) threatens a person's sense of security and self-worth (Brewer, 1991). It suggests that a high level of assimilation promotes deindividuation, or a minimizing of one's personal identity. This parallels the description of overidentification that I have associated with prejudice. In its original formulation, optimal distinctiveness leaves out the developmental and intrapsychic conditions that influence this process, and that may impede the countervailing need for differentiation.

In the optimal distinctiveness model, each dimension (differentiation and assimilation) is viewed as independent, yet interdependent. The more important the group becomes, the higher the level of deindividuation, and the more depersonalized the self-concept becomes. Brewer's model predicts that as one's sense of deindividuation increases, one's need for differentiation intensifies, and conversely as individuation increases, so does the need for assimilation. The optimal distinctiveness model stresses a level of inclusion in groups. Therefore the major emphasis is on the degree to which one is assimilated or individuated as a group member. *Optimal distinctiveness* refers to an ideal level of "equilibrium" such that any level of inclusiveness within a group activates equal needs for differentiation from, as well as assimilation with, the group (Brewer, 1991). In other words, equilibrium is achieved when inclusion needs are satisfied by assimilation within the group, and differentiation is satisfied by intergroup distinction (Brewer, 1999). Brewer's use of the notion of "optimal distinctiveness" never forgets that people are always functioning in relation to large groups.

Brewer's (2007) most recent formulation of optimal distinctiveness theory begins to stress the evolutionary implications of these needs. In this regard, she aligns optimal distinctiveness theory with a relational perspective. Brewer emphasizes the primary interdependence of group formation to survival, and highlights the role of separation and attachment needs in this process. From this perspective, ingroup favoritism makes sense as a basic motivator in personal and collective interaction. However, in contrast to social identity theory (discussed shortly), which explains this motivation as a product of self-esteem enhancement, Brewer redirects the focus to security needs as primary motivation for ingroup formation and favoritism. In contrast to social identity theory, positive evaluation of the ingroup becomes an outcome secondary to the survival need to belong to the ingroup. Optimal distinctiveness theory brings us much closer to coordinating the developmental, intrapsychic, and intergroup dimensions of human relations. The psychoanalytic emphasis on the survival motive is exemplified by attachment theory. The significance of integrating attachment theory into the discussion about intergroup relations and prejudice is just beginning to take shape and I will discuss the implications of this perspective to prejudice in detail in chapter 5. One relevant comment to the work by Brewer is that attachment theory is also concerned with equilibrium between autonomy and belonging, with prejudice being emphasized when attachment is threatened.

FROMM AND BREWER

Fromm's theory of deindividuation does not account for the prevalence of large group membership, and in a limited way suggests that the extent to which people are differentiated from the large group, in linear fashion, is a sign of psychological strength. We can say that Fromm's description of authoritarianism stresses an optimal balance between autonomy and loss of self (deindividuation) with preference in the direction of the autonomous individual. Fromm was most clearly interested in the authenticity of the individual and viewed large groups as structures used to compensate for personal limitations.

In the other direction, Brewer's view of balance, or equilibrium, stresses differentiation and assimilation as a group member. This perspective recognizes the functional relevance of group formation as an evolutionary component of our instinct to survive. The individual must balance needs for being part of the group with needs for being a unique group member. If we utilize both Fromm's and Brewer's discussions of deindividuation, we can more fully consider the relevance of separation and attachment processes for individual development in relation to other important individuals and also for the individual in relation to important large groups. Both models comment about the negative effect of deindividuation, as the individual merges with the large group.

FRUSTRATION-AGGRESSION HYPOTHESIS

In contrast to the effort to determine the pathology of the prejudiced personality, Dollard, Doob, Miller, Mowrer, and Sears (1939) provide a theory of normal human processes to explain prejudice. It is formulated in line with Freud's position on the pleasure principle in which frustration occurs whenever pleasure seeking or pain avoiding is blocked, and aggression is the result. In this frustration-aggression theory, if the agent of frustration is not functionally appropriate to aggress against, a substitute outlet will be found. This can occur through stimulus generalization, so that targets are similar to the frustrator. An example of this is the child who is bullied and takes out his or her aggression on other children. A second method of reestablishing equilibrium is through displacement. This method will find outlets for aggression that are unrelated to the original frustration. Dollard et al. (1939) thought that intergroup prejudice was a displacement of aggression from other ingroup members toward outgroups. This theory also utilizes Sumner's (1906) consideration of hostility between ingroups and outgroups, which Dollard et al. suggest implies that aggression toward the outgroup is a result of frustrations associated with competition for resources. The basic tenets of the frustration-aggression hypothesis are relational in that aggression is a secondary response. This psychoanalytic perspective about prejudice offers an interpersonal account for the hostile reactions between members of large groups. Work that continued to examine these dynamics began to incorporate a social learning perspective to account for other determinants of aggression. Frustration was acknowledged as creating a readiness to become aggressive, but targets would need to be safe to attack, strange, and already disliked (Hogg &

Abrams, 1988). It was also criticized for implying that if we can remove all frustrations in the world, there would not be any aggression (May, 1972). This theory did not receive continued attention from psychoanalysts and has not advanced from its original formulation.

YOUNG-BRUEHL'S MODEL OF MULTIPLE PREJUDICES

Elizabeth Young-Bruehl (1996) offers a psychoanalytic alternative to the limitations that arise by labeling prejudice as a mental illness, but maintains a categorical framework that may help to distinguish among variations of prejudice. She is a strong proponent for eliminating the perspective that prejudice is the same for each person. Instead, she directs our attention to the interrelationship between character of the individual and the targets of prejudice. She defines prejudice as a defense, and since different character types utilize defenses in unique ways, there are multiple prejudices. The extreme use of any defense is indicative of the pathology of the individual, and as such prejudice is pathological.

Young-Bruehl (1996) surveys the vast literature on prejudice, and she refreshes a psychoanalytic effort to examine prejudice after the field seemed to abdicate the study of prejudice to social psychology. She reintroduces the potential of the original efforts by showing that the psychological and sociological are interrelated. Young-Bruehl wants to avoid the limits of explanation that stem from either a macrosocial or individual differences perspective and dismisses the search for one underlying nature that can explain prejudice. Instead, Young-Bruehl espouses that prejudice should not be disassociated from the character of the individual, who is in turn bound to a given society that can restrict or unleash the prejudice of that particular character. In Young-Bruehl's theory she utilizes the psychoanalytic theory of character types (Freud, 1931; Reich, 1933/1972), which suggests that different characterological types have a unique developmental line and each relies on different defense mechanisms. Then she equates defense mechanisms and prejudices, which leads her to her central position, that if prejudices and defense mechanisms are the same, then we could expect differences in the way hysterical, obsessive, and narcissistic characters use their defenses, and thereby express their prejudices. Young-Bruehl stresses that we should acknowledge that different types of prejudices are enacted by different types of people, rather than one universal prejudice reflecting the same thing regardless of who or how it is expressed. Instead, the world provides targets to match the needs of the character type.

Young-Bruehl (1996; 2007) proposes three prejudiced personalities representing idealized personifications, whereas in reality there is much more variation. In the purified form, the obsessional character type will show rigid, moralistic, conventional, and often paranoid thinking. These individuals need to hoard, and are prone to be conformists. Splitting affect from intellectual operations is a major defensive style. This character type will be wary of conspiracies and so their prejudice could be directed toward Jews or Communists. They thrive in environments that stress discipline and order. The "authoritarian personality" is most closely associated with this type. A context of economic depression is most dangerous for unleashing the negative reactivity of these individuals.

A second character type is the hysterical character. This character dissociates and splits good and bad selves. This person, Young-Bruehl writes, could be a good upstanding citizen by day, and a racist by night. The environment that encourages this type include hierarchies in which one side is idealized and the other devalued. Young-Bruehl suggests that this type would associate prejudice with racist ideologies. A context that would allow free movement from one position in society to another threatens their security and therefore they react to conditions that equate groups.

The third character she examines is the narcissistic type. These individuals show grandiosity, and as such are preoccupied with superiority and inferiority. Their interest in beauty and body directs their prejudice in a sexist manner, and could be understood as an attack on what cannot be had. Narcissistic prejudice is oriented toward using the target for self-esteem maintenance. Young-Bruehl states that these individuals direct their prejudice at people they view as competition, which threatens their superiority. At the core of their anxieties, however, is a reaction about difference in gender. Young-Bruehl suggests that the narcissistic character turns to groups for a feeling of merger. This character type seems most closely associated with the potential to overidentify with the ingroup. Young-Bruehl may accept that overidentification with an ingroup is used for the purposes of security for the self. Ultimately, the narcissist is trying to deny differences, and when the other is not useful, they are nonexistent.

DIFFERENTIATING MODELS

Young-Bruehl offers a categorical model to understanding the variety of prejudices that are present in the world. The difference in approach with the current model may be in terms of emphasis, in which Young-Bruehl seems to differentiate between prejudices by recognizing the relevance of differences in the needs that are expressed by different character types. Importantly, her model does not attend to the implication of identity as a factor in the manifestation of prejudice between ingroups and outgroups. Instead, I suggest that the central feature in prejudice is collective identity, which she would consider a theory of ethnocentrism. Rather than categories that express prejudice, similar to the notion of phobias, the emphasis on the interrelationship of identity and prejudice is a dimensional model. By emphasizing the dimensional approach, prejudice is examined in terms of degree, or on a continuum from underidentification to overidentification with an ingroup. The developmental conditions that influence collective identity, the degree to which collective identity is salient for each person, and the various contexts in which it becomes more or less relevant become the focus for understanding prejudice.

DIFFERENTIATION AMONG CATEGORIES

Dalal (2002; 2006) emphasizes the role of power in understanding large group interactions. He argues that belonging to one category requires that another category exists to which one does not belong, and simultaneously only some may belong to the ingroup. The unavoidable result is that at the moment a person affiliates with a category, there is an automatic rejection of an "other" that does not belong to that category. The relational connotation of Dalal's analysis of categories involves an argument that in reality there are no distinctions between categories. In fact, he suggests that differences between categories are illusory, and concludes that actual differences are less important than the functions that processes of differentiation serve any person or group at any point they are emphasizing the difference. These differentiations reflect power relations between groups, and end up involving idealization of one's own and denigration of the other.

Many aspects of Dalal's work are congruent with this project; however, we attend to the relational implications in different ways. Although the categorizing process is automatic and through it we acknowledge that ingroups and outgroups are interdependent, Dalal's interpretation that attachment to the ingroup is an automatic rejection of an outgroup is an assumption about the function of the process. Rather than focusing on the outgroup to provide meaning for the attachment to the ingroup, I suggest that the attachment to the ingroup is the primary motivation. This ingroup favoritism does not come without consequences, one of which is that the outgroup may be discriminated against as the ingroup vies for status, self-esteem, and security. The necessary affiliation with an ingroup provides a specific category that facilitates collective identity. Dalal (2006) acknowledges that the conditions that facilitate ingroup belonging are necessary (e.g., presence of an outgroup and specification of who belongs to the ingroup) otherwise the resulting superordinate category would be so large that it is rendered meaningless. This is why I believe that the potential of a superordinate category, as an antidote for prejudice, is limited. It unfortunately cannot provide enough of the needed uniqueness that Brewer (1991) discusses in her optimal distinctiveness theory. For Dalal, the ingroup is artificially defined by the outgroup. He writes, "it is precisely because of the impossibility of finding and naming the essence of the *us* that one looks to the margins—to the *not us*." (2006, p. 150). An alternative relational meaning that I favor posits that belonging is an affirmation of self, rather than a rejection of the other. Consider the infant who attaches to her mother, and is oriented toward her mother, rather than someone else's mother. I think that in essence both mother and daughter are saying, "I am like you and this is how I know myself." The relational emphasis is on the progressive attachments that grow in what Allport (1954) calls concentric circles, and Fairbairn (1952) describes as extending from the family to the clan, tribe, and nation. Dalal's analysis is also true in that once ingroups are formed, they define themselves in contrast to the outgroup. However, if we are to seek methods of addressing the prejudice that is inevitable once ingroups and outgroups are formed, we must accurately understand the etiological factors that influence this process.

GORDON ALLPORT AND THE NATURE OF PREJUDICE

The politics between disciplines advocating an individual differences or intergroup processes perspective in the study of prejudice seemed to evolve over time. However, it did not start out that way, and early on these two approaches could inform and enrich each other about questions of mutual interest. The collaborative spirit in the work on the *Authoritarian Personality* was similarly inspired by the work of Gordon Allport. During the same period that the authoritarian personality was being formulated, social psychologists were also investigating the problem of prejudice. Gordon Allport's (1954) classic and still relevant book, *The Nature of Prejudice*, was written at a time when psychologists appreciated the potential for a psychoanalytically informed social psychology, or vice versa, a social psychologically informed psychoanalysis (Fromm, 1941/1963; Horney, 1939; Sullivan, 1964; Thompson, 1964). The subsequent fifty years largely neglected this potential, but perhaps it is becoming relevant again with the elaboration of a relational paradigm that currently permeates both psychoanalysis and social psychology.

Allport's highly influential book surveyed the field of prejudice and continues to inspire theorists and researchers. Allport accepts that prejudice is a problem of personality development in that prejudice reflects personal needs and habits; however, he was more interested in how the individual manifests the group's needs, rather than believing that groups reflect the individual's needs (the latter being more of a Freudian psychoanalytic position involving processes like projection). He writes, "it is possible to hold the individualistic type of theory without denying that the major influences upon the individual may be collective" (p. 39), and to this statement it is important to include the relevance of context.

Similar to how psychoanalysts return to Freud's original thinking about the inner world of people, as they build upon and redirect his insights and blindspots, so too do social psychologists interested in the study of prejudice return to Allport. In the last five decades social psychologists have broadened and advanced research and theoretical pursuits about prejudice, largely stemming from Allport's original work. In a recent survey of the field, Dovidio, Glick, and Budman (2005) pay respect to the sweeping influence Allport had, in the modern version, *On the Nature of Prejudice: Fifty Years after Allport.* As the table of contents of this contemporary presentation of the field indicates, the social psychological study of prejudice includes, from a contemporary vantage point, some of the psychoanalytic concepts that were acknowledged by Allport. The contemporary cognitive concepts more likely to be utilized by social psychologists are, "implicit cognitions" (unconscious), "nonconscious prejudice" (denial, splitting), or "well-rehearsed, internally consistent and socially validated justifications for group inequality" (rationalization). Could this be an indication that the days of a potentially overlapping social and psychoanalytic study of prejudice may be returning, albeit very slowly? All in all, regardless of the language, both fields are interested in engaging the psychodynamics of prejudice. Allport's position was skeptical, but not dismissing of psychoanalysis. Humorously he writes, "occasionally, we shall have to place strictures upon the exuberance of the theorizing . . . Yet this criticalness will not in the least diminish our indebtedness to Freud and to psychoanalysis" (p. 333, 1954).

The social cognitive perspective became the most dominant theoretical and research paradigm for the social psychology of prejudice, if not the study of prejudice overall. Allport's position is that, "dynamics of prejudice tend to parallel the dynamics of cognition" (p. 376, 1954). For Allport and social psychologists since the 1950s, the nature of prejudice and discrimination involves cognitive mechanisms that reflect normal human functioning (Dovidio, Glick, & Budman, 2005). The emphasis on normalcy should not be taken for granted nor overlooked as an important guide to understanding the pathology.

As is often the case, perhaps the evolution of our understanding about the dynamics of prejudice required sharp distinctions between individual-level processes and group-level processes. Now that each perspective is articulated, it is possible to discover the areas that overlap and can enhance the overall project. Clearly, it is not one or the other perspective that can solve the problem. Prejudice encompasses so much of human life, including intrapsychic, emotional, cognitive, interpersonal, and group phenomena. Although I would like to advocate for an interactive, mutually informative science between psychoanalysis and social psychology, I appreciate the need for and importance of a strictly group process-oriented science, as well as an individual-level, intrapsychically attentive psychoanalysis.

SOCIAL IDENTITY THEORY

In reaction to the dominant focus on individual differences, Henri Tajfel wanted to promote an approach that kept the large group central in social psychology by recognizing the constant effect of the large group in the mind of the individual. In the 1960s Tajfel began to develop Social Identity Theory, building on the work of Muzafer Sherif on intergroup conflict.

Sherif's (1961/1988) approach became known as Realistic Conflict Theory, and suggests that competition between groups for real resources and interests facilitates intergroup conflict, while simultaneously intensifying identification with, and positive attachment to, the ingroup (Tajfel & Turner, 1986). Sherif was able to conduct studies with boys who participated in a summer camp. Situations were arranged in which groups were formed to complete tasks with goals that varied the degree of competition and cooperation. Sherif reports that during competitive situations, ingroup cooperativeness increased. When tensions developed between the groups, ingroup solidarity increased. Intergroup relations were understood to be dependent upon the functional relations between them. When intergroup competition involved a goal that only one group can acquire, it led to hostility and negative labeling of the outgroup. The effort to change negative attitudes between the groups required much more than contact between the groups. Rather, tension was reduced when reciprocal cooperation was possible over tasks that involved mutual exchange of tools and responsibilities in meeting problems. Sherif introduced a series of superordinate goals that were compelling for both groups and required both groups to cooperate. This created a state of interdependence between groups that involved creating a plan and execution of the plan both groups developed. In order for intergroup relations to improve, repeated tasks with these superordinate goals had to be engaged. Still, there were individual members of the groups who wanted to return to the previous days of tension, though their voice was not very noticeable once the cooperative relations had been established. Could these individuals be the overidentified ones?

Picking up on the importance of the identification with the ingroup, Tajfel recognizes that the implications for intergroup relations could be better understood by clarifying the underlying processes that influence large group identifications. It was clear that the more intense the intergroup conflict, the more individuals in opposing groups will perceive each other as group members rather than individuals. This self-categorization process, very much a cognitive phenomenon, has important implications for intergroup relations (Turner, 1982). Much research has supported the initial insight that once people perceive ingroup belonging, they will accentuate similarities with other ingroup members, and also accentuate differences between the ingroup and outgroup members (Tajfel, Billig, Bundy, & Flament, 1971).

Social identity theory became widely influential and stimulated considerable research on group categorization and intergroup relations. It was shown that simply perceiving that one belongs to a group can trigger intergroup discrimination that favors the ingroup. Even when individuals are only participating in research and groupings are randomly assigned so that belonging to group "A" has no emotional value and there is no self-interest inducement, people tend to favor the ingroup in an effort to maximize differences with an outgroup (Tajfel & Turner, 1986).

Social identity involves part of an individual's self-concept that is based on perceptions of belonging to social categories (large groups). Tajfel and Turner (1986) write that the categories provide self-reference that defines one's place in society. Social identity theory suggests that people will strive to maintain or enhance positive self-evaluation and thereby make efforts to view their group positively, or better than relevant outgroups. Social psychologists in the United States tend to use the term collective identity when referring to this dimension of the self-concept, and I will continue with this term.

This approach is dependent upon the premise that categorization is an adaptive cognitive process that helps to simplify perception. Hogg and Abrams (1988) state that people classify other people in terms of similarity and difference, especially in relation to oneself as a reference. This implies that when certain social categories are important to an individual, it is always in relation to an outgroup. In the language of the authoritarian personality, this is the "contraidentification" with an outgroup member that they spoke about. The self-categorization process positions large groups in the mind of the individual. It is the basis of collective identity and why social identity theory suggests that people experience social relations to a great extent as group members.

Social identity theory promotes the idea that the ingroup can be part of the psychological self and a context that highlights collective identity minimizes differentiation between the self and the ingroup (Hogg & Abram, 1988; Smith & Henry, 1996). When this happens, the group represents the self. This is why individuals are motivated to evaluate their ingroup favorably, so that they can maintain self-esteem and self-worth. However, some people seem to maintain this perspective most, if not all, of the time. Such individuals would be similar to the authoritarian character described by Fromm, in that the self is subsumed by the group, and they will tend to view self and others as group members, regardless of context. In other words, their collective identity is salient all the time. Although this is a normal categorizing brain process, we can speculate that some individuals are compensating for a deficiency in self-experience. This perspective also gives some indication about how large groups of people can become collectively prejudiced toward an outgroup. For example, when societal conditions demand that people categorize themselves, others automatically become categorized as ingroup and outgroup members and perception in terms of similarity and difference is unavoidable. This can occur in transient situations like the camaraderie of tour groups (Hogg & Abrams, 1988), or collective identity will also be triggered if someone makes a racial slur (Mackie & Smith, 1998). It can also occur when societal conditions focus on large group tensions, such as during wars when people are on one side or the other.

RELATIONAL PARALLELS

Sumner (1906) believes that ethnocentrism is universal. His position suggests that ethnocentrism is a functional condition that influences group formation, as well as conflict between groups. However, the process by which the group becomes represented in the mind of a person is left unanswered. The work on the authoritarian personality suggests that the large group is a functional structure to which an individual attaches and works out intrapsychic conflicts. For example, the experience of self is dependent upon the group, and character influences the extent to which one will be dependent upon this external structure in order to function adequately as a person. At the time the authoritarian personality project was conducted, the relational perspective in psychoanalysis had not yet been elaborated. Today, the relational paradigm completely redirects the way we can speak about both pathology and healthy functioning.

Social identity theory moved social psychology in this direction as well, and in a significant way. For example, speaking of large group affiliations,

Tajfel and Turner (1986) state, "these identifications are to a very large extent relational and comparative: they define the individual as similar to or different from, as 'better' or 'worse' than members of other groups" (p. 16). The relational perspective in social cognitive psychology implies that we have a need for an ingroup. It also includes a developmental position. For example, Allport (1954) writes that the ingroup is primary because we establish a preference for the ingroup before we develop attitudes toward an outgroup. In particular, a relational paradigm suggests something about the findings pertaining to ingroup favoritism, in which people tend to report an interest in making their ingroup special without necessarily any animosity toward an outgroup.

In psychoanalysis, relational refers to the interpersonal nature of people, and the need that people have to establish satisfying relationships with other people (Fairbairn, 1952; Mitchell, 1988). The quality and importance of the relationship people have with large groups with which they affiliate, and thereby between their ingroup and people from outgroups, are only beginning to be considered in psychoanalysis. In my opinion this suggests that although ingroups and outgroups occur together by definition, emotionally we may have a need for an ingroup for security, but this does not necessarily imply that we automatically develop animosity for an outgroup.

The possibility for convergence between psychoanalysis and social psychology involves the influence of the relational paradigm. The mutual benefit this perspective can offer stems from the underlying motivational assumptions that this orientation highlights. Both disciplines seem to accept the position that people are oriented toward relationships with other people. This influences individual development and functional behavior within large groups. Central to this orientation are the conditions that facilitate or impede identification processes within an individual. In the study of prejudice, social identity theory shows how the strength of identification with a large group influences intergroup relations, but it is not a consistent finding that stronger identification with the ingroup is associated with more prejudice in the individual. Although, as we have said, behavior associated with favoring the ingroup is often associated with real world discrimination on a societal level. The psychoanalytic relational paradigm attends to developmental experiences associated with differentiation and identification that contribute to one's sense of self (Teicholz, 2006).

Taken together, both psychoanalysis and social psychology can provide a way to discuss the special condition of prejudice in more depth. This perspective engages the dialectical interdependence of one's personal developmental history and unconscious processes with the macrosocial conditions of the environment. The following chapter introduces overlapping conceptual schemes about separation and attachment processes from multiple disciplines. These dynamic forces function as the precursors of identity formation. Throughout development, a balance between separation and attachment, and the experience of autonomy or affiliation, is necessary (Aviram, 2007; Brewer, 2007). Culture plays a role here, by emphasizing one dimension or the other (Trafimow, Triandis, & Goto, 1991; Triandis, 1995). This is a common finding by cultural psychologists in that some cultures emphasize the autonomy dimension, while other cultures prefer the attachment dimension. As we progress toward understanding the underlying dynamics of identity, we are better able to address the group in the mind of the individual.

Chapter Three

The Group in the Person

A half century ago, Gordon Allport (1954) alluded to the relational motive in human nature. He stated, "Human nature seems, on the whole, to prefer the sight of kindness and friendliness to the sight of cruelty" (p. xiii). At that time, the relational perspective was only beginning to be formulated in psychoanalytic clinical theory by writers like Fairbairn, Guntrip, Sullivan, and Winnicott. Yet, Allport's comment is consonant with a movement that suggests that human behavior is motivated to establish and maintain satisfying and cooperative relationships with other people (Fairbairn, 1952). Mitchell (1988) writes, "The most useful way to view psychological reality is as operating within a relational matrix which encompasses both intrapsychic and interpersonal realms" (p. 9). The relational perspective in clinical work helps us to understand both health and pathology in the individual. If this premise is acceptable for clinical use, in order to address problems in relating among individuals, then it should be possible to extend this relational perspective to consider difficulties in relationships between groups of people. This is especially important if we proceed with the notion that large groups (identity groups) become represented in the mind of the individual, and the individual therefore may at times perceive people as members of large groups.

PREJUDICE AND LARGE GROUP IDENTITY

Our inquiry into the problem of prejudice can begin by identifying where it actually is a problem. This draws our attention immediately to large groups with which we all identify and that become part of each person's identity. The consequences of prejudice at the macrosocial level are evident in repetitive intergroup strife and destructive conflicts that continue to threaten people just about everywhere. Although we see the ultimate difficulties as large group phenomena, by understanding the relationship of the individual to the large group we may have more opportunities to minimize prejudice at its source. Large groups influence an important dimension of identity formation in the individual. Each infant is born into a context that ultimately shapes that individual. The influence of culture and large group structures of a given society facilitate an important dimension of the person that takes form in early adulthood when identity, and especially large group identity, is organized. Society requires that we become recognizable and offers a variety of classifications with which each person ultimately affiliates. There is no escape from this communal demand, for even the rejection of the larger community and its identity groups forces one into another sort of community and enables others to label, classify, understand, and predict behavior. Identity satisfies both individual needs for self-definition and societal needs for the integration of its members. Erik Erikson (1959/1980) discussed identity formation in similar terms. He writes,

> identity formation arises from the selective repudiation and mutual assimilation of childhood identifications, and their absorption in a new configuration, which in turn, is dependent on the process by which a society (often through subsocieties) identifies the young individual, recognizing him as somebody who had to become the way he is, and who, being the way he is, is taken for granted . . . For the community, in turn, feels "recognized" by the individual who cares to ask for recognition; it can, by the same token, feel deeply, and vengefully, rejected by the individual who does not seem to care. (p. 122)

Erikson's comment on "the individual who does not seem to care," draws our attention to the person who is experienced as "other." This person may not look like "us," or believe what "we" believe, and so on. In other words, he is not just like "us" and therefore he is one of "them." This outsider seems situated to be the recipient of prejudice.

Targets of prejudice and discrimination tend to be identified by some group-based feature such as nationality, religion, class, ethnicity, race, gender, sexual orientation, or countless other categorizations of identity. This natural tendency to categorize appears to be a universal cognitive process intended to simplify and organize the environment (Allport, 1954; Tajfel, 1969; Hogg & Abrams, 1988). However, a category only begins to contribute to large group identity (collective identity) when meaning is invested into the affiliation with the group (Keefe, 1992). At that point various categories are incorporated into the individual's self-concept.

ETHNOCENTRISM

The intensity of negative feelings, from dislike to hatred, that become inter-related with prejudice indicates that something terribly urgent is at stake. Because of the extreme reactions that can occur, Fonagy and Higgitt (2007) speculate that prejudice reflects an ontological question about Being. They are correct in that we need to recognize that in matters of prejudice the large group and the individual are intertwined so that survival of one represents the survival of the other. It is important to clarify how that occurs.

The literature on the role of large group identity in relation to prejudice was significantly influenced by Sumner's (1906) discussion of ethnocentrism. He introduced the terms *ingroup* and *outgroup* to delineate the large group boundaries that represent the individual's orientation to "this is mine" and "that is theirs." Sumner succinctly describes a theory in which the affiliation with a large group (ingroup) facilitates ongoing conflict with other groups (outgroups). Sumner states, "differentiation arises between ourselves, the we-group, or in-group, and everybody else, or the others-group, out-groups" (p. 12). Furthermore, he asserts that, "The relation of comradeship and peace in the we-group and the hostility and war toward others-groups are correlative to each other" (p. 12). Sumner believes that the differentiation that occurs between groups automatically leads to ethnocentrism and hostility between large groups. For Sumner, the more an ingroup is cohesive, the more the outgroup is rejected.

Research over the last century does not substantiate such a direct correlation between ingroup cohesion and outgroup hostility (Duckitt, 1992). Of course this relationship is complicated, but in general the intergroup condition may be more accurately depicted by a preference for one's ingroup, which tends to be a consistent finding and quite possibly may be universal (Brewer, 1991). Ingroup favoritism is not automatically associated with negative attitudes and hostility toward outgroups; however, functionally the hierarchies established in every society create power differentials between large groups that may ultimately facilitate hostility. Duckitt (1992) concludes that although the categorization and affiliation with large groups does not automatically involve outgroup hostility, as Sumner proposes, the situational conditions that highlight large group identifications do promote ingroup favoritism, which thereby facilitate the potential for prejudice, especially when environmental conditions, such as competition for resources or threats to the ingroup's value system, are present (Sherif, 1961/1988; Stephan & Renfro, 2003). Our consideration of prejudice as a secondary outcome stemming from ingroup favoritism is significant. It is the social psychological corollary of the psychoanalytic relational proposition that human beings are fundamentally oriented toward affiliation and attachment. Thus, the negative phenomena of prejudice and discrimination can be understood as compensatory and self-protective. Social psychologists have made significant contributions to this understanding of the relational meaning of prejudice.

An ethological example may provide perspective for this relational proposition regarding prejudice. Viewing the interactions between lions and hyenas may lead one to intuit that they hate each other. This anthropomorphic interpretation is based on the observation that when lions and hyenas confront each other they are likely to fight and try to kill one another. If we had no other information about their behavior, hate would be a logical explanation in our effort to apply an emotional connotation. This interpretation imposes a human perspective on behavior between two animal groups who fight with each other. However, if we allow ourselves to extrapolate from the animal world to our own, we may find an explanation for the destructive behavior of two human groups who "fight" each other. The two animal groups are not likely to resolve their animosity for each other, but this aggression involves their effort to survive in an unforgiving environment (Fromm, 1973). In essence the aggression may reflect a primary ingroup favoritism and secondary hatred for the other. Is this a possible explanation for prejudice in the human condition?

RE-DEFINING THE PROBLEM

A relational theory of prejudice directs our attention to the relationship of the individual with the ingroup, rather than his or her belief and attitude toward the outgroup. The focus is on the aberration of this interrelationship as the primary cause of prejudice. Prejudice is an outcome of an *overidentification* that has occurred between the self and the large group. This overidentification eliminates the distinction between the individual and the large group, and when prejudice is enacted, it indicates that fundamentally, for the prejudiced person, there is no difference between the individual self and the large group (Hogg & Abrams, 1988). This is a result of the effort to compensate for the inadequate security of the individual and ingroup. In this regard, the overidentification can be initiated from either position. In other words, prejudice indicates that at either the individual level or the intergroup level there is a perceived rational or irrational threat to the survival of the individual self and/or the ingroup. This may be influenced by developmental conditions or current situational conditions that impinge on the person. In the end, prejudice occurs among people who perceive themselves and each other as large group members rather than individuals.

Prejudice can also be discussed in terms of its emotional and/or cognitive elements. In its mildest attitudinal form it is a preference, while as a belief it can be a prejudgment. The most destructive expression of prejudice is a malignant compensation that involves fear and hatred of the dissimilar other. Hatred is a special case of prejudice that manifests as a consequence of the ultimate fragility of the self and the group, and incorporates massive use of the defenses of splitting, denial, and rationalization in order to maintain the idealization of the ingroup and devaluation of the outgroup (see chapters 4 and 6).

The use of psychological defenses infuses prejudice with both positive and negative attitudes and feelings about large social groups and their members (Mackie & Smith, 1998). These attitudes and feelings are directed at one's ingroup or toward outgroups. From this working definition it is clear that prejudice involves experiential states of self and beliefs about the self and others. Prejudice reflects beliefs and feelings that "I am one of these people," and at times an effort is made to enhance the status of the group. Simultaneously, there are beliefs and feelings about oneself as being different from and, at times, better than the outgroup. This bias tends to promote a simultaneous experience of "we are good and they are bad," or "I prefer these people over those people," whether or not these feelings are conscious.

Our effort to understand and define prejudice may be enhanced by our ability to articulate its opposite. The effort to identify the contrast to prejudice will lead us to clarify the optimal developmental conditions that could promote greater capacity to resist the pull toward prejudice. I will use Neil Altman's (1995) discussion of the related subject of values to move us in this direction. Altman (1995) states, "The challenge, then, is to believe strongly and deeply, without the assurance of an unquestionable foundation. This position amounts to taking personal responsibility for our moral commitments, as opposed to making appeals to universal validity" (p. 73). In Altman's comment we grasp the ideal, in which there is an optimal balance between personal conviction and absolute truth. We can apply this perspective to the relationship between the individual and the large group. During the course of development, the capacity for autonomy while experiencing attachment interacts in dialectic fashion. That is, human development entails becoming autonomous and being attached, and these two processes dialectically affect each other. This is vital in early development with caregivers, and these dynamics are also central during identity formation as the person forms relationships with large groups. The individual strives for an optimal balance between autonomy as a person and affiliation with the large group. It signals that our attention could focus on the developmental optimal management of separation and attachment processes and the relevance of these processes to large group identity. This is an ideal that provides a marker on the roadmap of development, and in essence provides a way to discuss the opposite of prejudice.

IDENTITY AND PREJUDICE

The concept of identity is a potential link between the psychoanalytic and social psychological explanations for prejudice. The literature tends to focus on either the individual person's pathology or societal conditions that affect intergroup relations. From either perspective, prejudice always brings the large group aspect of one's identity into consciousness, and this operates as a psychological bridge between prejudice as individually motivated, as well as influenced by intergroup conditions. For Erikson (1950; 1968), a crucial outcome of the identity formation process is that individuals can comfortably experience themselves as autonomous beings, and simultaneously feel part of the surrounding community as members of a large group. Erikson recognizes the importance of a conceptual balance between separation and attachment processes. This is crucial for personal well-being in relation to other people, and serves a similar purpose for the individual, as one begins to identify with large groups. Ultimately it will be necessary for psychological disciplines to collaborate in order to understand the complexity of the interrelationship between the individual and the group. Yet psychoanalytic and social psychological efforts have rarely informed each other since the initial major efforts that studied prejudice following the Second World War. Perhaps this is an enactment of the very subject under study.

RELATIONALITY AND PREJUDICE

We should be impressed by the capacity of people from different cultures and societies to get along. This is most apparent when one travels and encounters differences in the social structures and customs that vary around the world. It is at those times that our shared humanity becomes most apparent. Our capacity to attend to similarity, rather than difference, is most striking when we ask for directions, order a meal, or laugh with a stranger in a foreign land. That is not to say that differences are not real, but it is important to acknowledge this cooperative potential at the beginning of a discussion about prejudice. It suggests that an examination of the problem of prejudice in the context of a relational theory of human nature may provide new insights.

Allport took notice of our capacity for affiliation and the common human potential for cooperation regardless of differences. This is important to remember when we are discussing a corresponding truth in our capacity for prejudice toward seemingly dissimilar others. When I travel I am often reminded of Harry Stack Sullivan's one genus postulate, which states, "we are all more simply human than otherwise." I am impressed by the personal and simultaneous global implications of this phrase. It suggests that with all our differences we are all basically attending to common human needs. The truth of this postulate, however, becomes more complicated when we perceive others or ourselves as members of large social groups. This is because we are all dependent upon, and susceptible to a categorizing brain process that necessitates our differentiation from others. This categorizing process can be essentially neutral, such as when we differentiate between salt and pepper. However, categorizing can become significantly value laden. It is a basic cognitive mechanism that facilitates identity formation. Categorizing is fundamental in helping us understand who we are. It binds us to particular groups of culturally similar people, and simultaneously serves as a point of reference from which we see ourselves as different from others. The problems associated with prejudice are essentially dependent upon this categorizing process and identity.

We can ask if and how this fundamental need to discriminate between things in the world, which contributes to a basic human need to understand who one is, becomes the basis for discrimination against the other, the outsider. This is a tragic human story in that, to discover who we are and develop our identity, we will forever be in potential conflict with other people who we believe to be "different" from ourselves. Sullivan's postulate reminds us that it is an essential human need to establish collective identity, and part of identity formation involves affiliation with other people. The irony may be that the very act of establishing identity and affiliation with one group of people promotes differentiation and potential hostility with others. How this basic human need to discriminate between categories leads to the social tragedy of prejudice and discrimination will be explored in this book.

A PERSONAL ANECDOTE

When I was in my early twenties I had just completed serving in the military in Israel and I immediately ventured out to experience my regained freedom by traveling. Partly because of proximity and partly curiosity and interest, I began my travels in Egypt. Although Israel and Egypt had signed a peace treaty a few years earlier, I was conscious that I did not want to advertise my Israeli identity. Since I grew up in the United States I presented myself as an

American. This allowed me to feel safer, though nothing had changed except my own perception about my group affiliation. The people I met were warm and hospitable, and I could not help but be aware of the potential of interpersonal relations and peace between nations. On my taxicab ride to the airport I was having a friendly chat with the driver when he asked where I had been, and I told him in Israel. I asked him what he thought of Israel and he made a negative remark about the Israelis. Probably feeling emboldened to address the subject as I was leaving, to his surprise I told him that I was Israeli. My guess is that he had never met an Israeli. He acknowledged that he meant the government's policies and not the people. I mention this incident in order to point out the fluid and perceptual implications of large group identity (Dalal, 2002).

From Cairo I flew to Athens where, after a day or two, a charismatic Israeli expatriate living in Athens recognized me to be Israeli because of the sandals I was wearing. These were typical sandals that at that time were very popular in Israel. By the way, I wore them throughout my stay in Egypt. Something this man said struck me powerfully, and I was immediately and lastingly impressed. He said, "You know there are many Palestinians here in Athens." I was wondering why he was telling me this, and perhaps responding to a concerned look on my face, he continued, "But there is nothing to worry about, we are not in Israel." That was a profound statement. I asked myself, "Why don't I have to worry in Athens, but I do in Israel?" Prejudice is a complicated subject, but one that involves large group identity and context. At times, collective identity will override context and influence the course of prejudice for an individual. At other times, the context will influence one person's experience of identity, or even affect a whole group of people, as these stories indicate, and could lead to prejudicial behavior that may not arise in another context.

In the remainder of this chapter, I will discuss evidence from diverse disciplines in psychology that highlight overlapping concepts about separation and attachment needs in development and identity formation. This will provide the foundation to understand the model of prejudice that will be described in the remainder of the book. Collective identity is always salient when prejudicial behavior occurs, and therefore a discussion of the developmental precursors to large group identity is necessary. In early development, the notion of an optimal balance of separation and attachment dynamics with caregivers is crucial. Similarly, in early adulthood, balance of these same dynamics influences one's experience of autonomy, and the simultaneous capacity to affiliate with the large group. Both psychoanalytic and social cognitive efforts to understand this process have important implications for the study of prejudice.

EARLY DEVELOPMENT AND IDENTITY

In the last few decades, the emergence of a relational perspective in developmental theories (Bowlby, 1969; Chodorow, 1978; Mitchell, 1988; Stern, 1985) has provided an important point of view that informs multiple levels of human functioning. This shift in perspective has its roots in object relations theory, suggesting that infants seek contact and affiliation with the caregiver (Fairbairn, 1952), and that an experience of self develops in relationship with other people (Rubens, 1994). Relational theories are important in the evolution of the study of infant development and have balanced classical notions that emphasize an infant's need to experience psychological growth in terms of separation and individuation from an initial symbiotic attachment with the caregiver (Mahler, Pine, & Bergman, 1975). The classical perspective considered relationships to be secondary goals in development. For drive theory adherents, the infant uses significant people in his or her life to gratify instinctual drives associated with biological and psychological needs. The relational perspective reversed the view of motivational factors in an infant. Relationalists suggest that an infant seeks to connect with another human being from the beginning. Rather than needing to psychologically differentiate oneself from a caregiver, the infant seeks the nurturance of the relationship, and drives assist in this process.

It is necessary to clarify the roles of both separation and attachment dynamics in development. In early life, as well as throughout the lifespan, it is important to feel one has a sense of psychological autonomy, while simultaneously experiencing a sense of affiliation, connection, and belonging. This matters with relevant individuals, as well as large groups. Different societies and cultures may emphasize one dimension over the other (Triandis, 1995); however, extremes in one direction or the other are likely to affect psychological well-being. A conceptual framework, in which both separation and attachment are prominent psychological needs, provides a precursor to understanding how identity formation can potentially have equivalent influence on intrapsychic, interpersonal, and intergroup dynamics in early adulthood (Cooper, Grotevant, & Condon, 1983; Grotevant & Cooper, 1986).

The necessity of managing autonomy and attachment needs in early life foreshadows a similar requirement when we affiliate with large groups in society. Once again, a balance of autonomy and attachment with the group is a necessary process. The relevance of the separation-attachment dynamic is evident from the broad discussions that have emerged from several disciplines in psychology, such as (1) from a family systems perspective: fusion-differentiation-cutoff (Bowen, 1978), and enmeshment-disengagement

(Minuchin, 1974); (2) from a psychoanalytic perspective: interpersonal re-latedness and self-definition (Blatt, 1990), symbiosis and separation-individuation (Mahler et al., 1975), and connection and autonomy (Benjamin, 1995); and (3) from a social cognitive perspective: assimilation and differen-tiation (Brewer, 1991) and personal identity and collective identity (Luhtanen & Crocker, 1992).

The following discussion will address the emergence of separation and at-tachment as central concepts in theories of early development. It will become apparent that promoting either separation needs or attachment needs as pri-mary goals in development emphasizes only a partial view of our psycholog-ical needs. The growing recognition of interdependence and the importance of promoting balance between autonomy and affiliation expands the range for consideration about identity formation and the eventual implications con-cerning interpersonal and intergroup relationships.

SEPARATION AND ATTACHMENT IN EARLY DEVELOPMENT

The psychological interdependence between separation and attachment needs manifests in a preference for closeness or distance in relationships. This dy-namic remains important throughout one's lifetime (Benjamin, 1995; Holmes, 1996). It is likely that the effect of this psychological interplay has enormous influence on personality development (Blatt & Shichman, 1983; Blass & Blatt, 1992), which in turn determines a certain level of functioning in the world. Most efforts to understand development describe the relevance of connections with others, as well as the importance of a sense of autonomy from others (Blass & Blatt, 1992). Each theoretical perspective, however, is aligned with certain philosophical notions about the development of self (Mitchell, 1988). These positions reflect a conceptualization of the develop-ment of self on a linear trajectory that either begins from a psychologically undifferentiated merger with a caregiver thereby promoting a need to sepa-rate, or conversely, entering the world with some awareness of self and other, and needing to psychologically establish an attachment with a caregiver in or-der to survive. Most notably from a psychoanalytic developmental perspec-tive, Mahler and her colleagues (1975) have come to represent the classical position advocating separation as a developmental goal. A decade later, Stern (1985) introduced widely influential infant research suggesting that develop-ment is dependent on the potential to establish attachments (relationships). Stern's work is part of a broad literature that includes the psychology of women and object relations theories and is regarded as part of the relational perspective (Greenberg & Mitchell, 1983).

MARGARET MAHLER AND SEPARATION-INDIVIDUATION

Mahler, Pine, and Bergman (1975) open their classic book by making it clear that they believe that normal adult functioning is dependent upon the experience of being "both fully in, and fully separate from, the world out there" (p. 3). However, their premise is dependent upon a view of "psychological birth" as a process of separation-individuation. This process refers to "the establishment of a sense of separateness from, and relation to, a world of reality, particularly with regard to . . . the primary love object" (p. 3). Although Mahler and her colleagues mention the importance of the "relation to" the caregiver, their notions are based on the idea that a sense of being, or what they call "identity," is dependent upon normal separation-individuation. As a result, the relational aspect of their framework is not elaborated because they presume a given over-relatedness (symbiosis).

This influential perspective acknowledges the importance of separation and attachment in the development of self; however, the emergence of a self is perceived to follow an initial period during which intrapsychic differentiation between self and caregiver has not taken place. As one separates from the caregiver, there is greater emphasis on personal aspects of self as different from the caregiver, rather than the common features shared by both the individual and the other person. As a framework that places central importance on independence and autonomy as primary features of self, this perspective is reflective of Western values. The pendulum did swing to the other side in an effort to represent aspects of self-development relevant to Eastern values, feminist ideologies, and sociological traditions.

THE RELATIONAL PERSPECTIVE

Encouraged by psychoanalytic developmental research with infants, which began to offer evidence that did not support Mahler's hypothesis regarding a symbiotic phase, researchers speculated that infants are aware of "being in the world" from the beginning and thus seek to establish attachments with caregivers (Stern, 1985). This reversal of the primary goal in development gained strength from a variety of sources.

John Bowlby (1969), an early proponent of the relational model, integrated a large body of evidence suggesting that infants seek attachments with caregivers. He discusses ethological findings suggesting that newborns and parents of all species, including humans, quickly learn to distinguish themselves from other newborns or parents that may be in the same proximity. Human infants may take up to three months, he suggests, to respond differentially to a caregiver and noncaregiver, although more recent studies suggest that even human infants have an almost immediate ability to distinguish between their mother's and another woman's breast milk (Stern, 1985). Here we see the initial efforts to discriminate between "my mother" and other mothers. Bowlby advocates for notions such as Fairbairn's (1946/1952) that we are motivated to establish satisfying relations with other people, shifting the emphasis from a purely intrapsychic process to incorporate an interpersonal motivation for psychological growth.

SEPARATION OR ATTACHMENT: EXTREMES

Elaboration of a relational model provides the perspective needed before the importance of both separation and attachment dynamics could be appreciated as necessarily interdependent influences during development. The views of several writers, each with his or her unique emphasis, share a common view that an optimal balance between separation and attachment needs is necessary for healthy psychological development. Extremes in one direction or the other can lead to pathology.

Jessica Benjamin (1995) discusses this dynamic in terms of "recognition." She states that at the moment an infant realizes that he or she has independent will, dependence emerges on another person for recognition. From an intersubjective perspective, Benjamin (1995) proposes that the ideal resolution of this paradox is that it continue as a constant tension between "recognition" by important others and "self-assertion." She places the responsibility on the caregiver to adequately respect the infant's need for independence. "Recognition" acknowledges the importance of the relationship and provides the security from which to pursue independence. Relevant to our discussion, if the attachment between the caregiver and infant is inadequate, then "recognition" of the infant's need for separation would not be possible. This is a hint about the potential influence of early development on identifications with large groups. When there are problems with caregiver attachments, Benjamin (1995) states that what is needed is "to balance assertion and recognition" (p. 38), or risk continued dependence in which omnipotence is attributed to either the caregiver or the self. Lack of balance between separation and attachment needs when we affiliate with large groups will have similar implications.

Sidney Blatt and his colleagues (Blatt, 1990; Blass & Blatt, 1992; Blatt & Shichman, 1983) discuss how attachment and separation influence personality development in terms of interpersonal relatedness and self-definition. Blatt (1990) states that "an increasingly differentiated, integrated, and mature sense of self is contingent on establishing satisfying interpersonal experiences, and conversely, the continued development of increasingly mature and satisfying interpersonal relationships is contingent on the development of more mature self-definition and identity" (p. 299). Importantly, in normal development, these processes evolve in an interactive and balanced fashion throughout one's lifetime (Blass & Blatt, 1992; Blatt & Shichman, 1983).

Undoubtedly, biological predispositions or environmental insults can influence the development of one line over the other. Even within the normal range of development, Blatt (1990) states that individuals could emphasize one developmental line over the other. We could further suggest that culture will influence one line over the other. In Blatt's work, each dimension describes a broad personality type, and these personality dimensions are related to two broad configurations of psychopathology. Blatt and Shichman (1983) describe such personality types as either "anaclitic," who tend to focus on interpersonal relatedness, or "introjective," who are organized around self-definition. In relation to psychopathology, anaclitic disorders are "distorted and exaggerated attempts to maintain satisfying interpersonal experiences," while introjective pathologies are distorted and exaggerated efforts to establish an "effective concept of the self." Blass and Blatt (1992) acknowledge the dual aims of both attachment and separateness in similar fashion to Benjamin's (1995) description of "recognition" and "self-assertion."

SEPARATION AND ATTACHMENT: IDENTITY FORMATION IN ADOLESCENCE

For most of the last century, limitations of developmental theories had hindered a complete consideration of the identity formation process (Erikson, 1968). For example, Blos (1967) saw parallels between the identity formation process during adolescence and earlier efforts to separate and individuate during infancy and early childhood. His model is based on a classical psychoanalytic view that the infant is psychologically merged with a caregiver and struggles to separate and experience autonomy from that caregiver by internalizing the parent as a constant object. From this perspective, identity formation initiates a "second separation-individuation process," in which the adolescent is again struggling to gain autonomy from parents, literally, but also from internalized infantile object relations (Blos, 1967). The notion that adolescents recapitulate the earlier separation-individuation process during identity formation was a general premise of identity theory and research.

Additional empirical work in this area, however, has failed to completely support the separation-individuation process in identity formation. Rather, researchers found that adolescents who had achieved a sense of identity also reported ongoing relationships with their parents (Cooper, Grotevant, & Condon, 1983; Grotevant & Cooper, 1986; Rice, 1990). Recent evidence suggests that in cases of normal development, a continuous relationship with parents persists from childhood through adolescence (Grotevant & Cooper, 1986; Palladino-Schultheiss & Blustein, 1994; and Rice, FitzGerald, Whaley, & Gibbs, 1995). However, taken to the extreme, this perspective minimizes the actual changes that may occur within the parent-adolescent relationship in terms of autonomy (Grotevant & Cooper, 1986). It is important to recognize that focusing on either a separation-individuation process or an attachment process by itself only illuminates one dimension of the real relationship between adolescents and significant others. The preceding discussion indicates how separation and attachment dynamics in early life provide the foundation to address identity formation in adolescence and early adulthood. It is at this stage that affiliation of the individual with large groups in society demands that the dynamics of separation and attachment remain relevant.

A SOCIAL COGNITIVE PERSPECTIVE ON IDENTITY

Gergen (1971) proposes that the self could be described in terms of categories that people attribute to internal and external aspects of themselves. This has been further delineated as the self-concept that includes the totality of self-identifications, or self-descriptions and self-evaluations, available to a person (Hogg & Abrams, 1988; Turner, 1982). Self-identifications tend to divide along two dimensions or subsystems of the self-concept called personal identity and social identity (Hogg & Abrams, 1988). Personal identity refers to self-identifications that are idiosyncratic, such as traits and attributes like intelligent, competent, anxious, or hardworking. Social identity refers to the dimension of the self-concept that contains self-identifications related to membership in social categories, and the roles that stem from them (Gergen, 1971; Hogg & Abrams, 1988).

Personal identity and social identity emerge consistently in studies that ask about one's self-concept (Kuhn & McPartland, 1954). These types of self-identifications have also been consistent descriptors cross-culturally, although culture may influence an emphasis on one dimension or the other (Trafimow, Triandis, & Goto, 1991; Triandis, Bontempo, Villareal, Asai, & Lucca, 1988). In the United States, social psychologists have introduced the term "collective identity" to refer to aspects of the self-concept that pertain to large social groups, while the term "social identity" is reserved for aspects of the self-concept that reflect interpersonal domains (Luhtanen & Crocker, 1992). These basic dimensions of the self-concept reflect individual uniqueness in terms of personal identity, or group affiliations in terms of collective identity. In keeping with current terminology, collective identity will be used to describe identity associated with large social groups and social roles, such as nationality, religion, sex, race, father, or teacher.

ADVANCES IN SOCIAL COGNITIVE THEORY ABOUT COLLECTIVE IDENTITY

Social psychological research on self-esteem provides support for examining the interdependent development of personal and collective identity. Although not discussed directly, these concepts parallel the separation and attachment dynamics that have already been discussed. In fact, we can speculate that perhaps the development of personal and collective identity are manifestations in early adulthood of the previous management of separation and attachment needs.

Luhtanen and Crocker (1992) suggest that the importance of belonging to an ingroup may be moderated by self-esteem. These researchers propose that self-esteem can be enhanced or diminished by the large groups to which we belong, especially if collective identity is important to the person. This suggests that self-esteem associated with personal identity, and that is associated with interpersonal relationships, is separate from, but interrelated with, self-esteem associated with collective identity, which is dependent upon large group affiliations. Cases of extreme dependence upon one identity dimension seem to be indicative of a compensation for a weakness in the other identity dimension, with implications for one's global sense of self. In such cases an underlying deficit in the self is being corrected by means of an overidentification with one identity dimension or the other exclusively.

Direct evidence for such compensation has been reported. Ng (1989) posits a model that states that "although [personal identity and collective identity] are structurally distinct, functionally they may be mutable so that the loss to the overall self-concept due to a deficiency in one component can be compensated for by a gain in the other" (p. 6). Ng introduces this model to account for findings of bias in reward allocations given to both ingroup members and outgroup members by study participants whose group status was manipulated and identified as inferior (Ng, 1986). He suggests that bias functioned to safeguard either personal identity or collective identity when one dimension is deficient. He found that this compensation worked in both directions to protect or enhance self-esteem (Ng, 1985).

Additional evidence is available about the independence of either the personal identity or collective identity dimensions. Robins and Foster (1994) found that when feedback about the status of one's group was manipulated to be low, subjects with high collective self-esteem showed an increase in favoritism toward the self as compared to the group. When group status was low, collective identity did not contribute positively to the self-concept. People without high collective self-esteem tended to favor the self, regardless of their ingroup status. Robins and Foster (1994) speculate that individuals who have high collective self-esteem, implying that group affiliations are important to these individuals, are especially dependent upon their large groups to gain a positive self-concept. These individuals are more likely to try to enhance their collective identity if the group's positive qualities are threatened. Alternatively, when group enhancement strategies are unsuccessful or not available, they may abandon their group identification altogether.

Maintaining self-esteem is considered to be a normal motivating force that is sustained by accentuating positive qualities of the ingroup for comparison with an outgroup, and minimizing negative dimensions for comparison (Turner, 1982). As a result, people are motivated to positively evaluate their ingroup, and by implication, enhance their collective self-esteem. It appears that whenever a group affiliation is made salient and meaningful, one's collective identity will influence behavior in an effort to maintain collective self-esteem. This is predicted by social identity theory (Hogg and Abrams, 1988). However, people vary under normal circumstances in the degree of importance they place on collective identity. Individuals who report a strong emphasis on collective identity are prone to take measures to protect their collective self-esteem in relation to outgroups, even when a threat is not apparent. Furthermore, collective self-esteem appears to be interdependent with personal self-esteem. In other words, each dimension may compensate for the other.

LIFESPAN PERSPECTIVE ON SEPARATION
AND ATTACHMENT DYNAMICS

Conceptually, identity may be an integrating link between the psychological and social psychological explanations of prejudice, providing a scheme for understanding prejudice as intrapsychically motivated, as well as influenced by the context and intergroup conditions. Current knowledge regarding separation and attachment dynamics indicates that the subjective experience of needs for separation and attachment influences the development of personal and collective identity, and that this process may continue throughout one's lifetime in an interdependent fashion. At both early and later stages, it appears that balance is most appropriate. Early development involves interdependence between separation and attachment dynamics with significant caregiving figures. It is possible that the quality achieved in managing separation and attachment dynamics throughout one's life influences how one relies upon personal identity and collective identity. For example, a preference for closeness or distance in personal relationships may be associated with the degree to which one is able to affiliate with groups in adulthood in both conscious and unconscious fashion. Being overly dependent upon the group, or conversely, not being able to feel that one has a place in a group, is likely to be indicative of underlying emotional needs that affect functioning. Just as in early development, the ability to experience balance, or equilibrium, between personal identity and collective identity may be optimal in adulthood. An exaggeration of personal identity, or collective identity, beyond some threshold, may indicate a problem in the subjective experience of self, and may indicate difficulties with underlying separation and attachment dynamics. A developmental perspective attends to early influences on an infant that could have lifelong consequences for self-esteem. Combining theory and research from psychoanalytic developmental psychology and social cognitive psychology highlights that some individuals may need to sustain a positive view of their ingroup in an effort to overcome deficiencies in personal self-esteem stemming from early life relationships.

Erik Erikson provides further theoretical impetus to continue to seek convergence between disciplines. In the broadest terms, his description of ego identity may be understood as a scheme for the self (Erikson, 1968). The developmental process that ultimately results in the establishment of "ego identity" lies at the border between psychology and sociology, or the individual and his or her relationship with the surrounding community (Erikson, 1959). Erikson predicts that advances in developmental theory would offer the framework needed to integrate information from diverse perspectives into a coherent psychosocial theory of identity.

THE PSYCHOANALYTIC WITH THE SOCIAL PSYCHOLOGICAL

Studying the interrelationship between identity and prejudice involves both intrapsychic and macrosocial considerations and therefore we can benefit by incorporating both psychoanalytic and social cognitive approaches. A successful convergence of ideas has the potential to inform our understanding of the development of self, group behavior, and the interaction between the individual and the large group.

Developmental theories have stimulated research that is changing longstanding notions regarding the concept of identity (Blatt & Shichman, 1983; Bowlby, 1973; Chodorow, 1978; Gilligan, 1982). Specifically, consideration of both separation and attachment needs helps to provide a more complete understanding of the individual's development. The importance of balancing needs for closeness with needs for autonomy, in relation to caregivers during early development, is now recognized as essential to psychological well-being and to healthy identity formation in early adulthood. Clinically, extremes of either separation or attachment are indicative of pathology. An example was discussed earlier in terms of introjective and anaclitic personalities.

Psychopathology is associated with a lack of boundaries between oneself and significant others, or overly rigid boundaries and an inability to form lasting relationships altogether. Similarly, the association between personal identity and collective identity dimensions of the self-concept may also be associated with psychological well-being. An emphasis on either personal or collective identity suggests a compensation for a weakness in the other identity dimension. This may indicate difficulty in establishing oneself as a unique and functional individual during interpersonal situations (personal identity), and concurrently developing a sense of belonging and affiliation with important large groups (collective identity). As such, when there is a problem with personal identity, one may compensate by over-identifying with a group to enhance collective self-esteem. Conversely, when an individual has difficulty maintaining a connection with an identity group, he or she may compensate by trying to bolster personal identity. Such cases may occur when one belongs to a stigmatized group and identifying with the group has a negative impact on collective self-esteem (Aviram and Rosenfeld, 2002). An ability to experience affiliation with societal groups and institutions, while also maintaining a sense of uniqueness, may depend on the outcome of the developmental effort to balance separation and attachment needs with caregivers at an earlier period.

Establishing collective identity is a necessary developmental process that provides a sense of belonging in society. This is an important process in all cultures. It is predicated on an individual's ability to experience autonomy (personal identity) while also experiencing group belonging (collective identity). If we accept that prejudice is dependent upon one's degree of identification with a large social group, then we are in a position to examine the interpersonal (individual differences) and societal (contextual) conditions that influence this process. In this sense, prejudice is ubiquitous and naturally occurring and may be on a continuum from underidentification to overidentification. On one end of the continuum would be the individual who could not identify with people or large groups. A person with schizophrenia would represent this end of the continuum. On the other end, the overidentified individual, we have someone who has merged with the large group. This is the individual who is prejudiced toward the outgroup regardless of context, though anyone could find that they are moving in this direction when the context ascribes large group distinctions to individuals and may impose consequences because of group membership. There is a paradox in all this. It calls to mind the saying, "if you travel far enough to the east you end up in the west." Here we have two ends of a continuum, but both individuals have lost their individual self. The person with schizophrenia is apparently unable to hold onto a sense of self, and the prejudiced person has merged the individual self with the large group.

The precursor to prejudice as a pathological condition is rooted in the developmental management of separation and attachment needs in early development. Ideally, individuals balance needs for closeness and distance in their relationships with caregivers. During identity formation this process reemerges, as individuals struggle to manage closeness and distance needs with large groups in society. However, as will be discussed in chapter 4, the group is not merely a parental substitution. The large group begins to have its own influence on intrapsychic experience that may not parallel object relations associated with important individuals in one's personal history. An overidentification with an identity group represents a compensation for deficiencies in the experience of self and is interdependent with early experience, as well as current context. The extent to which an individual is identified with the ingroup will determine the degree to which he or she is able maintain the ideal optimal balance between autonomy as an individual and affiliation with the large group.

IMPLICATIONS FOR THE STUDY OF PREJUDICE

Psychoanalytic inquiry was originally most concerned with the intrapsychic condition of the patient without regard to the context of treatment or the influence of the psychoanalyst. Only later was this initial approach identified as a one-person psychology. It slowly changed as psychoanalysts began to value the relevance of the environment in contributing to pathology. This shift in awareness about the process of psychotherapeutic engagement recognizes that both the analyst and patient are significant contributors to the experience of psychoanalysis. Today this perspective is broadly identified as a relational psychoanalysis. In the clinical context it acknowledges the mutual influence of both the therapist and the patient as contributing to the process of change. From today's vantage point, this trajectory seems logical as the field advanced.

We can anticipate that if this progress continues, then the evolution of ideas in psychoanalysis will incorporate the role of the large group in the mind of the individual. In other words, we can see how the original focus of inquiry in psychoanalysis proceeded from an initial interest primarily in the inner world of the patient, to then include context and the actual relationships in the patient's life, including the therapist, and ultimately it should bring the large group into the session by recognizing that culture and large group affiliations cannot be left outside of the consulting room. Although psychoanalytic writers have made some contributions to the study of the large group (Bion, 1959; Foulkes, 1948/1983; Hopper, 2003; Volkan, 1988), this area has not been sufficiently integrated with the available knowledge about individual psychology. Furthermore, because the role of the large group in the mind of the individual has not been well formulated in psychoanalytic theory, efforts to describe sociological phenomena, such as prejudice, have been limited and psychoanalysis has even been dismissed for not being very helpful in understanding societal problems. The deserved criticism reflected the lack of appropriate attention to the social, political, historical, and economic factors that affect intergroup relations and facilitate prejudice (Bettelheim & Janowitz, 1950). The relational perspective has been a major development in psychoanalytic contribution to understanding the human condition, and today can help us address societal problems in new ways.

There has been a tremendous amount written about prejudice within psychoanalysis and social psychology. Each body of writing can stand on its own. In developmental theory, when the capacity to consider the interrelationship of separation and attachment dynamics became possible, advances in theory and research proceeded. Similarly, the effort to study prejudice will be advanced if we can attend to the interrelationship of these two literatures, paying attention to the interpenetration of the intrapsychic and the macrosocial. The following chapter elaborates an object relations theory of prejudice and considers an intrapsychic process that is present as the individual forms a relationship with the large group, placing the large group in the mind of the individual.

Chapter Four

Object Relations Theory of Prejudice

Toward the end of Freud's life psychoanalysts were beginning to elaborate the object relational implications that were present in his writing, but were undeveloped. This relational perspective attends to the interactional patterns that evolve between the self and others (Mitchell, 1993). Object relations theories flourished throughout the remainder of the twentieth century, with varying degrees of emphasis upon the intrapsychic implications of interpersonal functioning. For example, Fairbairn (1952) was primarily concerned with internalized object relationships, and real interpersonal relations that were represented in the unconscious. Sullivan (1953) was more interested in the actual relationships and limited the relevance of the unconscious during treatment. Kohut (1971) focused on the self and the impact of relationships for self development, which involved unconscious process and experiences of deficit, and understood the self in a very different way from Fairbairn. In general, psychoanalytic models emphasize the well-being of the individual in relationship with other individuals. Consideration of the systemic influence upon the well-being of the person has had some attention, but it has been difficult to ascertain how psychoanalysis can clinically attend to the impact of the surrounding community (Fromm, 1955; Sullivan, 1964; Kohut, 1985). Treatment providers seem to be uncertain about how to utilize cultural or large group dynamics during psychotherapy and psychoanalysis. This does not mean that it is irrelevant. Instead it indicates that there is much more to understand, and that the system within which the individual functions is a relevant topic for psychoanalysts to consider further.

FAIRBAIRN'S OBJECT RELATIONS THEORY

Fairbairn's object relations theory is the clearest psychoanalytic framework that elaborates an intrapsychic place for the actual relationships in a person's life. Fairbairn (1952) writes that identifications with other people facilitate the emotional experience of self. In other words, we gain an experience of self through our interactions and affiliations with significant people in our life. This is usually associated with caregivers and other important relationships in early life; however, there is no reason to discount influences of these kinds of relationships throughout one's life for better or worse.

Intimate relationships reflect our emotional needs in managing separation and attachment processes, or experiences of closeness and distance during interpersonal relationships. Fairbairn saw this in terms of degrees of dependence between people that are unavoidable and natural. For Fairbairn, development proceeds from complete dependence upon the caregiver, which he called infantile dependence, to a more interdependent position that he called mature dependence. There is a constant tension between a desire for dependence, and a defense against the loss of self that would commensurate with complete dependence. Fairbairn believes that infantile dependence minimizes differentiation between the self and another significant person. Intrapsychically this is facilitated by primary identification, which is the earliest form of identification. In Fairbairn's theory, pathology reflects the "persistence into later life of an exaggerated degree of that emotional dependence which is characteristic of childhood" (1952, p. 259). So pathology is an indication that primary identification continues to influence interactions. In contrast, mature dependence is characterized by the capacity to have "cooperative relationships with differentiated objects" (p. 145). Differentiation is never a complete process, and therefore no one is expected to be free of these early identifications. This has important implications later in life when we form adult relationships. Therefore, if identification facilitates the experience of self, increasing degrees of dependence imply that one's experience of self is dependent upon the other to a greater extent. Separateness is likely to be experienced as vulnerability.

OBJECT RELATIONS AND LARGE GROUPS

We can consider whether in the transition into adulthood, the degree of emotional identification with early objects influences the degree of emotional identification possible, or necessary, with large groups in society. This is an important proposition because it allows us to extend Fairbairn's notion and suggest that identifications with large groups can also begin to influence one's experience of self (Aviram, 2002; 2005; 2007). It is potentially meaningful with any large group with which one develops an emotional identification. Fairbairn could see that the original social identifications in the family influence subsequent identifications. This should not be limited to one category, but rather involves identifications with a variety of societal and cultural structures such as religion, gender, class, sexual orientation, gangs, professional categories, and numerous additional social structures with which one can identify. We will need to clarify how the process of identification that occurs between a child and caregiver, and later between adults, can extend to large groups. It is at this large group level that prejudice manifests, and therefore our understanding of the identification process that extends to large groups must be further explained. An individual's developmental history can account for this in some cases. It is also possible that macrosocial conditions can affect many people simultaneously and potentially initiate a temporary aberration in the identification process.

Just as identifications with individuals proceed on a continuum, so too it is possible to discuss identifications with large groups as developing along a continuum from minimal identification to overidentification. The degree of identification with a large group can influence behavior in an intergroup setting. For example, individuals engage with their ingroup at different levels of intensity, which can also vary at different times. This can be represented by a common situation in an ethnically diverse high school lunch room, where teenagers tend to congregate with ethnically similar peers, but with minimal consequences for intergroup relations. Further along the continuum could be the recent vote in France and the Netherlands, which rejected the proposed European Union Constitution, one reason for which was a reaction to a threat of losing the specialness of being French and Dutch. The implication here is that if you are not part of the ingroup, you may not be welcome. Having possible greater intergroup consequences, we may consider a recent vote in Iraq, in which each ethnic group voted for the candidates of their own ethnic group. In this case, the intergroup tensions are apparent, and potential violence organized around belonging to one group or another is possible. At the extreme is the pathologically prejudiced person, overidentified with his or her ingroup, and less likely to be influenced by situational variables. In the three preceding examples, the context could affect just about anybody present. This last condition does not depend on context to influence the degree of identification. Rather, this is an individual-level condition that is interdependent with the environment, but is intrapsychically driven. This individual is overidentified with his or her large group as a compensation for developmental conditions.

OVERIDENTIFICATION AND PREJUDICE

Fairbairn's object relations theory proposes that adult psychopathology reflects an infantile dependence, which is associated with primary identification. This defensive process served a protective function in early life, but in early adulthood it can influence the identity formation process as individuals form psychological and emotional relationships with large groups. In these cases the early defensive process of primary identification continues to affect one's experience of self during the identity formation stage. The potential to overidentify and minimize differentiation between the self and other persists, and may facilitate an overidentification between the self and group. This overidentification is associated with the psychological experience that minimizes differentiation between the self and the large group. When this occurs the large group and the self are identical from a psychological perspective. This kind of interdependent relationship between the self and large group is also espoused by social identity theory (Hogg & Abrams, 1988) and depicted in Fromm's (1941) authoritarian personality. To answer the question of why prejudice can emerge from this psychological condition, it is helpful to elaborate the developmental implications of identification.

The first identifications occur in the family. Fairbairn (1935/1952) perceives the family to be the original social group upon which the child is dependent. This is a psychoanalytic parallel to Allport's proposition that the ingroup is primary, and outgroups are perceived only after the ingroup is psychologically established. Ultimately, identifications with family members extend beyond the boundaries of the home to what Fairbairn (1935/1952) termed the clan, tribe, and nation. These are the identity groups of proximity or ancestral inheritance. Here we see that he recognizes that the necessary and sufficient degree of dependence and identification established with early love objects continues throughout life, and evolves to include the groups that are available in any given society. These social structures become our identity groups and are internalized. We can call these large group internalizations social object representations, with which emotional identifications continue with societal structures. This will be addressed shortly in detail. Although Fairbairn did not discuss this directly, the transition proceeds from some quality of dependence upon parents to some quality of dependence upon the large social group.

In our effort to understand prejudice, Fairbairn's description of psychological maturation is helpful. Healthy development involves mutual dependence between the individual and early love objects. A transition from infantile dependence to mature dependence is facilitated when caregivers offer genuine love, and accept such love back from their child. Under these conditions, healthy development is a process whereby relationships become more differentiated, yet continuously involve a mutual dependence. By extending this process forward from early childhood, it would also apply to the relationship between the individual and the large group. If earlier stages of development "persist" along with primary identification and infantile dependence, the young adult is handicapped in forming the new large group identifications in a mature dependent fashion. The large group can end up being used in an effort to compensate for the deficient sense of self that is associated with the infantile character. Primary identification continues to function as the defensive operation promoting an overidentification with the large group. This is the intrapsychic process that facilitates prejudice between the ingroup, which has become identical to the self, and outgroups.

The adolescent phase highlights the normal developmental potential of the identity formation process. This maturational process occurs in a condensed period of time and helps us understand the relationship between the self and large group. Erik Erikson's (1959) description of the adolescent identity formation process provides a snapshot of the potential overidentification with a large group that occurs during adolescence. He states that youths may:

> temporarily overidentify, to the point of apparent complete loss of identity [self], with heroes of cliques and crowds . . . they become remarkably clannish, intolerant, and cruel in their exclusion of others who are "different" in skin color or cultural background. (p. 97)

Erikson (1959) suggests that this behavior is an adaptive defense in adolescence against a sense of identity confusion. Bettelheim and Janowitz (1950) carry this observation beyond adolescence. They note that the need to overidentify with the group is a compensation for a weak sense of personal identity, or self. It is a compensation to avoid the emotional strain of identity confusion or total loss of identity.

FAIRBAIRN'S STRUCTURAL MODEL AND THE LARGE GROUP

There is an irony associated with prejudice in that when we reject a person due to his or her large group affiliation, we declare and locate ourselves firmly within a different group. There is no escape from large group membership, and therefore no escape from being the victim or perpetrator of prejudice, often both. The interplay between an idealized and powerful self in relation to a devalued and weak other is well depicted in Fairbairn's structural theory. He elaborates an intrapsychic model that is based upon actual relations with caregivers. Psychologically the infant is oriented toward relating to whatever kind of caregiver is present. Given the initial complete dependence upon this caregiver, the infant needs to protect the goodness and value of this external object. Unavoidably, when an infant cannot cope with unsatisfying aspects of experience, Fairbairn's "central self" splits into what he called the libidinal and antilibidinal egos (selves). This structuralization of the self constitutes a kind of pathology of the self. The more extensive and profound the splits are from the central self, the more extensive and profound is the resultant pathology (Rubens, 1994). In other words, the more disturbed the early environment, the more the infant will have a psychological need to push the actual experience with the caregiver into the unconscious. As this occurs the external world becomes simplified into good and bad objects.

The implications for prejudice are clear. In this model, there is a need to perceive the object upon which one is dependent as good. If we accept that pathology is associated with primary identification that persists into adulthood, there is an implication that the split of the central self into libidinal and antilibidinal selves has occurred. The question to ask is to what extent? During early adulthood the developmental task involves another set of identifications, this time with large groups. However, the capacity to establish these identifications must be influenced by the preestablished capacity to identify on the continuum from infantile dependence to mature dependence. Now, in early adulthood, the internal environment (unconscious), rather than the external environment (as was the case in early development), will determine the degree of identification with the large group. The extent to which there is an overidentification with the ingroup, the more there will be a need to experience the ingroup as good, and the outgroup as bad.

Fairbairn's writing was just beginning to attend to the implications of the psychological and emotional development of individuals in interaction with large group structures. He applied his model to political regimes and military authority to explain the potential of these organizations to compensate for inadequate psychological and emotional development. Similarly, he commented upon the way the political structure associated with large groups can manipulate or shape individuals within a society to conform and replace the concept of self as an individual with the self as a group member. Writing during the Second World War, Fairbairn noticed that a small proportion of soldiers psychologically collapsed after a short time in the army. Contrary to what we might expect, these soldiers were strongly identified with the military. So why did they breakdown? Fairbairn suggests that these individuals depended upon the military as a compensating organization, in similar fashion to previous dependence upon their caregivers. In other words, these soldiers could be said to have a "persistence of infantile dependence" that became associated with the large group, as it had been with early caregivers.

The description of these soldiers is important because they appear to represent individuals with a predisposition to establish a strong psychological identification with a large group (in this case the military). He reports that these soldiers "were so consumed with military zeal that they itched impatiently to be at the forefront of the fray" (1952, p. 278). Their pathology is revealed, however, when they have psychological breakdowns, following the military's rejection of their enthusiasm. We can speculate that these soldiers were eager to engage the enemy-outgroup. As long as their idealized ingroup compensated for their weak sense of self, they were able to function. However, in time the military's awareness of their zealotry, rather than simply being patriotic, led to caution. The withdrawal of the attachment by the authority deflated their overcompensated attachment to the idealized group, at which point psychological health deteriorated.

Further evidence that Fairbairn was beginning to recognize the relevance of large group identifications is found in his discussion of totalitarianism. He suggests that totalitarian regimes such as Nazi Germany and the USSR developed State-sponsored propaganda to foster an overidentification from the population as a whole (1952, p. 284). This is an example of an externally driven, context-influenced condition, as opposed to the previous example, which is internally driven. Such identification would promote a dependence upon the State as a substitute for familial bonds, and foster infantile dependence at the macrosocial level. In these kinds of regimes, security is fostered by belonging to the ingroup, while aggression is directed at outgroups. Fairbairn could have recognized that in a democracy individuals are less dependent upon the State, but still may be vulnerable to the development of overidentification, particularly in times of insecurity. Exactly how these large group identifications are represented in the mind needs to be addressed. As may be anticipated, important questions arise as to our understanding of large groups as either parental substitutes or as new and independent object representations that can influence behavior and perception in additional ways, and different from traditional object representations.

LARGE GROUP IDENTIFICATIONS

Attending to cultural and identity group affiliations has been relevant in psychoanalysis from the beginning. Freud (1921) thought that variations between groups reflect intrapsychic structures. For him, society reflects self. Contrastingly, theorists like Sullivan (1953) and Fromm (1955/1966) attended to the independent contribution of society and culture and stressed an interactive process that unfolds between individuals and their environments, each influencing the other. From this perspective, self reflects society. We can see that the position we take will influence our reflections about how large groups are to be represented in the mind. The former view indicates that by the time large groups become important, object relations of interpersonal relationships are sufficient to understand the role of the large group. The relational perspective suggests that large groups can have new meaning and influence on the person. The mind must be able to represent the large group in new ways that are interdependent with pre-existing experience, but sufficiently independent to reflect the uniqueness of the large group. The argument for creating a language for the large group in the mind must be further elaborated.

The additional emphasis on society and culture requires that we evaluate whether current conceptions of object representations adequately account for a person's large group affiliations and intergroup relations. It seems to me that traditional conceptions of object representations may need to be augmented to account for cultural and social group affiliations. This would emphasize that large social groups become incorporated as social object representations (social objects) and could independently influence perception of the social world. It would clarify that affiliations with large social groups, consciously experienced in terms of collective identity, can also have an intrapsychic role in addition to traditional object representations that reflect interpersonal relations.

During early adulthood the developmental task requires that identity groups become relevant and may stimulate new intrapsychic processes that are influenced by pre-established object representations associated with figures of personal historical significance (Blos, 1967). These identity groups now become the external social objects with which emotional identifications continue. This process may begin much earlier in life, especially for minority individuals (White, 2002). This may be a result of a continuous exposure to one's ascribed category by the majority, as well as familial reaction to the majority in a society.

For the most part, the young adult's affiliation with the large group has been understood as a parental substitution (Blos, 1967). This view is closely linked to the classical perspective that social groups are projected manifestations of intrapsychic process. Although Fairbairn had a relational emphasis for his theory, he too did not adequately differentiate the role of large groups in the mind. By simply extrapolating from Fairbairn's theory, it is not clear that large group representations are not akin to parental substitutions. Today, we are able to examine this more thoroughly. As individuals develop and their dependence needs include social groups, it is important to consider if the degree of identification is a recapitulation of earlier identifications with primary caregivers, or if these identifications can also reflect separate and new processes that independently influence the emotional experience of self and other. If social groups are considered to be parental substitutes, as Freud, Blos, and others suggest, than the elaboration of a social object construct, as an intrapsychic representation of one's relationship to the group, as well as one's position during intergroup conditions, may not be necessary or useful. In that case, current conceptions of object relations would allow us to understand one's relationship to the group as parental substitution. However, I would like to further consider if and how the concept of the social object representation can be clinically useful.

THE SOCIAL OBJECT

Hopper (1996) states that the mind is "real" even though it cannot be touched, and we can extend this to say that the large group in the mind is also "real." We must begin with Fairbairn's (1952) notion that identifications with caregivers contribute to the emotional experience of self. Given that as young adults we develop identifications with large social groups as we establish collective identity, Fairbairn's notion can be extended to include large social groups that also can influence one's experience of self. The question that follows this extrapolation is whether identifications with groups are equivalent to identifications with important individuals from one's past. The following evidence from social psychology indicates that identifications with large groups may be separate, but interrelated with object relations associated with individuals.

Social psychologists have described two dimensions of the self-system that they call collective identity and personal identity. During intergroup conditions we are likely to experience ourselves as group members, making collective identity salient (Hogg & Abrams, 1988). Personal identity is more relevant during interpersonal situations and is organized around traits and attributes of the individual. The traditional description of object representation may be more applicable to the interpersonal context, in which personal identity is highlighted. We should consider whether social conditions that highlight collective identity promote a different experience of self-as-group-member, rather than as an individual. If so, this would suggest that the object representations that facilitate an emotional experience of self-as-group-member might be separate from the object representations related to identifications with important figures from one's own past.

Additional evidence supports consideration of a social object as a separate intrapsychic process. The two identity dimensions of the self-system have been linked to two dimensions of self-esteem. Luhtanen and Crocker (1992) have shown that personal self-esteem can be enhanced or diminished by personal identity. This dimension of the self-system operates during interpersonal situations. Collective self-esteem is associated with social group affiliations and the intergroup context. From this perspective, personal identity affects personal self-esteem and is associated with personal traits and attributes. Collective identity affects collective self-esteem and is related to large group affiliations and roles in society. These are two separate, but interdependent, dimensions of the self-system. From a psychoanalytic perspective we can surmise that when collective identity is salient the social object will have greater influence on self-as-group-member experience and collective self-esteem, and therefore perception and behavior toward similar and dissimilar others as ingroup and outgroup members. The social cognitive literature is quite interesting and important for psychoanalysts to consider as we attend to the societal and cultural influence on the treatment process.

The relevance and impact of the broader society upon the individual, and between individuals, is receiving renewed attention as immigrant populations become increasingly numerous and seek psychoanalytic treatment (Altman, 1995; Cushman, 1995; Leary, 1997; Akhtar, 1999; Hamer, 2002; Hopper, 2003; Bodnar, 2004; Walls, 2004; Bonovitz, 2005; Dalal, 2006). Identifications with large groups can be recognized in the mind as social object representations that are interdependent with, but qualitatively different from, object representations associated with interpersonal relations. This construct provides a way to speak about environmental conditions that can influence behavior in ways that would not be anticipated if traditional object representations associated with individuals are considered alone. The social world and large group phenomena can overwhelm individuals and influence their behavior. Individuals behave far better or far worse as group members than they may be able to as individuals. These behaviors are not readily explained by traditional conceptions of object relations. There are many examples of altruism, and just as many of horrific acts when collective identity is salient. These are group-influenced behaviors that are highly affected by collective identity. This is associated with behavior that discriminates against others based on large group identity, such as nationality or ethnicity. We evaluate group belongingness during times of social instability, such as when one is a victim of discrimination or racism, however, such evaluations also occur under less stressful conditions, for example, when we meet someone from a different identity group. During these intergroup situations collective identity may automatically become salient (Hogg & Abrams, 1988) and influence self experience as a group member. The prejudiced person is influenced by the unconscious aspects of large group membership regardless of the situational factors just described. The social object concept allows us to ask how the large group in the mind influences behavior.

Social groups, and importantly the individuals who make them up, may be perceived in simple idealized fashion, or contrastingly devalued. Research in social psychology indicates that during intergroup situations, group members become de-personalized and individuals take on group attributes with homogeneous qualities (Verkuyten & Hagendoorn, 1998). This may facilitate or interfere with healthy identification, or attachment, with certain people or groups. Fairbairn's model explains this in terms of the nature of the subsidiary selves (libidinal and antilibidinal selves), which eliminate the complexity and/or imperfections of objects (Rubens, 1994). This is one explanation of how perception of others as group members reduces individual variation into homogeneous perceptions of others. It seems to involve splitting defenses of idealization and devaluation in order to manage interpersonal relations, along with differentiation between self and other, and likewise self and group. When individuals perceive themselves and others as large group members, they differentiate the ingroup and outgroup. Whether we use Fairbairn's endopsychic model or not, the social object representation can help clarify the implications of identifications with large societal groups. When collective identity is salient, perceptions of ingroup or outgroup status of individuals have been affected by identification processes. This is the potential condition when the patient and therapist are from different identity groups, but also when they are from apparently similar identity groups. How large group identity is triggered in the mind is a relevant consideration.

MACROSOCIAL CONSIDERATIONS IN CLINICAL WORK

The meaning of the patient's collective identity, in relation to the therapist's, adds an important dimension to the psychotherapeutic task. The Diagnostic and Statistical Manual-IV (DSM-IV, 1994) devotes a section to cultural formulation and culture-bound syndromes. The manual states, "it is important that the clinician take into account the individual's ethnic and cultural context in the evaluation of each of the DSM-IV axes" (p. 843), and notes that diagnostic assessment "can be especially challenging when a clinician from one ethnic or cultural group uses DSM-IV classification to evaluate an individual from a different ethnic or cultural group" (p. xxiv). Efforts to establish a productive working relationship during psychotherapy may be influenced by the collective identity of each participant. Relatively little attention has been given to collective identity as a co-determining variable associated with process and outcome in treatment. Furthermore, in the broader psychotherapy community, discussions about culture or ethnicity in psychotherapy often address nonverbal communication, or cultural styles and preferences, with almost no attention being given to unconscious processes that may influence such interactions.

CULTURE AND IDENTIFICATION

Allport (1954) believes that perceptions of boundaries between one's ingroup and outgroups could be more or less inclusive depending on individual needs or social conditions. If Allport's formulation is accurate, it could have important implications when considering the process of identification between two individuals who are members of different identity groups in a context such as psychotherapy. This suggests that in certain contexts, or between certain individuals, the ingroup/outgroup distinction may be less salient, and the necessary identification with the therapist may be possible, regardless of group membership and cultural differences. In contrast, there may be some individuals who may not be able to minimize identity group distinctions so that interpersonal relations are affected by perceptions of group differences (Aviram, 2002), and this could shape process in psychotherapy. Allport's formulation indicates that a conception of a continuum may be relevant when evaluating group identification processes. At the extremes of the continuum, individuals would be underidentified or overidentified with groups. Exploring conscious awareness about group identification processes and similarities and differences between the patient and therapist, in terms collective identity, provides a recognizable and meaningful heuristic that ultimately may offer an opening for understanding the impact of culture and society in the unconscious. The function of a social object representation will be described in the context of a clinical treatment that may offer a way of addressing the cultural and large group dimension in the unconscious.

CLINICAL ILLUSTRATION

Mr. Marquez is a single, gay, Latino male in his mid-forties. He is dependent upon his partner for financial support and shelter. Mr. Marquez had a history of drug and alcohol use beginning in his teens, with a period of sobriety for several years, followed by periodic slips with crack-cocaine and alcohol. He complained of depression and isolation from friends and family. During his early life he felt neglected by his parents and siblings. We were unable to adequately understand the reasons for his experienced rejection. He has felt like an outsider throughout his life, and found temporary relief for his longing to be accepted through transient identifications with a variety of identities.

These included other drug and alcohol users, homeless persons, as an unemployed adult, and as a gay male. His family was poor, and his parents were uneducated, placing them at the fringe of society. His family's struggle as immigrants was difficult, and seems perpetuated in his own story. He experienced barriers that perplexed him, and he had little ability to determine the extent to which these limits were self-generated, in relation to societal constraints.

THE SOCIAL OBJECT IN MR. MARQUEZ'S INNER WORLD

In the first session he made it clear that he did not want to be labeled with a diagnosis. Instead, he lectured about psychology and how labels are imposed unfairly. The first moments of our meeting were dominated by perceptions of group membership and struggle for power. I tolerated the position that engendered feelings of powerlessness or helplessness, and hypothesized that it was his way of communicating his experience in the world. Mr. Marquez was telling me that he has abilities that should not be overshadowed by his psychological struggles, or his ethnicity, social class, sexual orientation, or any other group affiliation that can label him. Simultaneously, he was seeing me as a particular kind of person based on my role as psychologist, Caucasian, apparently wealthy, and powerful. In other words, he was seeing me as a group member, which overshadowed any effort to be a person with him.

This is an example of how the social object representation can become intertwined with traditional object representations associated with historical figures and influence perception in individuals when collective identity is salient. Our interactions often left me feeling unimportant, devalued, and sometimes threatened. In an effort to emphasize the self-as-group-member perception, and the impact on self-esteem with which it is associated, I could have addressed these moments by asking: "When you think I may be judging you, are you experiencing both of us as particular kinds of people; me as the White psychologist, you as the Latino patient?" Another question might be: "It seems that it's not simply people who can be hurtful, but the group the person is part of, that makes a difference. How is that affecting our relationship?" If I understand my experience with him, and his reactions to me, solely in terms of traditional object relations (early caregiver experience), I may overlook that his capacity to relate is filtered through perceptions of people as group members. This is relevant because collective identity can be used to compensate for negative self-worth stemming from early object relations (Ng, 1985; 1986), but it also places others in deindividuated roles as group members.

We can consider if and how societal group dynamics play out between individuals during psychotherapy and how the social object can be clinically useful as a separate construct that is interdependent with traditional object relations. Mr. Marquez grew up in a deprived environment, with caregiving figures who were experienced as neglectful and unloving. His hopelessness about improving his life, being accepted by other people, and being a productive member of society stems from his early experiences, as well as his current social milieu. His (personal) self-worth is significantly compromised by his poor social position as an inadequately functioning person. However, he seeks temporary enhancement of (collective) self-esteem by affiliating with certain identity groups (Aviram & Rosenfeld, 2002, Marmarosh & Corazzini, 1997). In his particular case, he seems to cling to an idealized "outsider" identity that he uses both defensively and to bolster his self-esteem as he devalues others from "insider" groups. We can speculate that his object representations that are associated with parental and sibling figures keep him isolated and hopeless about being accepted by others. Consideration of his social object representations provides an additional perspective.

The concept of a social object draws attention to the dynamic interaction between identity groups and the inner world. The social objects in Mr. Marquez's case seem to continuously highlight his collective identities and offer him a place to stand from which he evaluates others. Importantly, the social object representation must have been influenced by his early object representations associated with early life relationships with important others. In our sessions he stated his concern about my being White, educated, and a professional. He fantasized that I have all that he wants. He feared that I will misunderstand him, or worse, judge and devalue him, and simultaneously he hoped that therapy would be able to help him find a way to move forward in his life. After several months he reported that he had been on several job interviews with no offers. His disappointment led to increased depression and he cancelled several sessions. Upon his return, he directly discussed the difference between us, in terms of ethnicity and opportunity, the limits he faces in the world, and concerns that those same limits will be imposed in our work together.

It is also relevant to note that the therapist is not only being perceived to belong to certain large groups, but actually does have particular collective identities and therefore social objects that are affected by the patient. Attending to the therapist's experience is commonly addressed in today's clinical literature in terms of countertransference. Significant efforts are made by clinicians to attend to the conscious aspects of this process. The therapist's ability to bring into focus the experiences that reflect the interaction as it pertains to large group dynamics offers a possibility of recognizing the macrosocial in the interpersonal. When discussion about differences or similarities emerges, or when idealized or devalued others appear in all good, or all bad, terms, I often find that one's group experience is latent. It is an indication of an overidentification and reflects a prejudiced perception regarding the therapist and/or other people. This is similar to Hopper's (1996) discussion of a "social unconscious" that is the repository of cultural and large group meaning in the mind, and which can be gleaned from the content patients offer about significant others. Opportunities to attend to perceptions and experiences related to collective identity can become central at those moments, and could include perception of the clinician as an outgroup member or an ingroup member. This is perhaps an unavoidable condition of a cross-cultural, patient-therapist dyad, and is present, but perhaps more subtle, with superficially similar dyads. The emotional effect of the social object is reflected in the emphasis on the self-as-group-member experience and collective self-esteem. It is here that the boundary between the self and group can become conscious. The extent to which one is more or less merged with the group significantly influences perception of ingroup and outgroup members. For some individuals this is largely dependent upon early object relations and character formation; however, environmental conditions also influence perception of collective identity and can more or less blur the self-as-group-member boundary for most, if not all, people.

At times, Mr. Marquez was overidentified with certain group identities, usually intensifying when he felt personally vulnerable. At those times he was not only differentiated from me, but felt unrelated, different from, and maybe threatened by our relationship. Our efforts to speak about these interactions were strained, but I believe also provided a way for him to understand the experience of rejection that he frequently encountered. In addition to addressing characterological constraints and repetitions, it is possible, at certain times, to attend to actual social conditions that operate in society and manifest through conscious aspects of collective identity and collective self-esteem. In addressing the unconscious aspects of large group identifications, the therapist can comment upon the oneness between self and group, or the idealized and devalued splitting that is being described. From this perspective Mr. Marquez devalued me and simultaneously felt strong as a group member, while avoiding the interpersonal dynamics of rejection and longing to be cared about as his early experience would also predict.

COMMENTS ON THE USE OF PSYCHOLOGICAL DEFENSES IN PREJUDICE

It has been reported that people accentuate differences between themselves and outgroup members (Tajfel et al., 1971; Verkuyten & Hagendoorn, 1998).

This suggests that the defense mechanisms of splitting and massive denial are pervasive when prejudice is active. Prejudice involves the capacity to keep the good and idealized ingroup quite separate from the bad and devalued outgroup. It suggests that the self and the other are perceived as part objects, rather than whole objects that include good and bad elements. One question that arises is, if an individual uses denial to maintain a self-perception of being good and belonging to a good identity group, is it necessary to set up a bad outgroup that can be perceived as less than oneself? Historically, this was often explained in terms of projection of unacceptable parts of oneself (Newman and Caldwell, 2005). The parts of oneself that cannot be tolerated Sullivan called the "not-me." Projection is a convenient psychoanalytic mechanism that explains this process; however, it does not satisfactorily explain the actual intergroup dynamics that are dependent upon an ingroup always being in relationship to an outgroup (Hogg & Abrams, 1988) and the actual competitions that impact intergroup relations. If it is so, that we have a primary need for an ingroup but not necessarily for an outgroup, part of the answer to the question I pose suggests that a negative bias toward an outgroup reflects additional defensive mechanisms that are self-protective (Young-Bruehl, 2007). If we accept that splitting and denial are functional psychological defense mechanisms that also facilitate prejudice, we can think further about the interpersonal implications. The result of viewing outgroups as bad and less than ingroups denies the less desirable components in oneself. Prejudiced individuals and groups of individuals tend to focus on particularly negative and devaluing aspects of the other, and positive aspects of themselves. The self-enhancement motivation posited by social identity theory is one explanation for this compensation, and so is Brewer's (2007) contention that ingroup favoritism is linked to security needs.

The Roman playwright Terence (c. 190–158 B.C.E.) insightfully declared, "nothing human is alien to me." Prejudice seems to promote a perception and emotional reaction to the outgroup in which the other is quite alien. It indicates that the functional psychological defense of splitting is present, in which the prejudiced individual is consciously attending to only one dimension of the ingroup and its opposite in the outgroup. It facilitates the perception of the ingroup and self as good, while the outgroup and its members is bad. Denial furthers this perception by eliminating the possibility of badness in oneself and not recognizing the positive in the outgroup. Importantly, these defense mechanisms, splitting and denial, also permit perception of actual aspects of oneself and other people. It is in line with Terence's awareness that all people possess both good and bad qualities that can be recognized within oneself, but these defenses eliminate whole-person perceptions. In contrast, projection implies that the negative that is perceived by the prejudiced person in the outgroup member essentially involves projected unacceptable aspects of the prejudiced person. It does not account for more complete perceptions of people as possessing both good and bad qualities.

I am suggesting that in studying prejudice, it would be better to acknowledge that all people can recognize the admirable and the repulsive precisely because they are human qualities. This is in no way a justification for blaming the target groups of prejudice for the animosity that is directed at them. Rather, it acknowledges that each outgroup is an ingroup for its own members, and in turn has an interrelationship with outgroups. Splitting and denial defenses, more so than projection, reflect the simultaneous potential of good and bad in humanity. As a means of acceptance of the sometimes contradictory and inaccurate perceptions that emerge with splitting and denial defenses, individuals further rationalize their beliefs. This becomes most evident when stereotypes are discussed. All of these defensive processes are in service of protecting and enhancing self experience. Prejudice is one mode in which the individual, or the large group, employs extreme means in order to protect the self and ingroup. The implications for psychotherapy and psychoanalysis are evident, given that these defenses are as ubiquitous as prejudice is, and it seems prejudice is bound to these kinds of defenses (see chapter 6). The following section will expand these ideas by including some of the parallel modes for understanding these problems in the social cognitive literature.

OVERLAPPING CONCEPTS IN PSYCHOANALYSIS AND SOCIAL COGNITIVE PSYCHOLOGY

Stereotypes are simplifying beliefs that cannot be overlooked in this discussion. Allport highlights the interrelationship between social categories and the fixed ideas that accompany them. Jost and Hamilton (2005) point out that stereotyping is an efficient means that permits further justification of cultural and institutional prejudices. Stereotypes are belief structures about large groups and their members based on expectations that are learned early in life and influence perception in adulthood. Jost and Hamilton (2005) summarize several decades of research findings about stereotypes. They indicate that stereotypes direct attention to certain information, influence the interpretation of that information, affect how that information is retained in memory, and shape judgments and actions, which thereby promotes behavior by the perceiver that can elicit additional behavior from the target person that confirms the perceiver's biases. This last point is essentially the self-fulfilling prophesy, which also has a rich research history. It is also strikingly descriptive of the influence of object representations from the psychoanalytic tradition.

Harry Stack Sullivan (1953) discusses an unconscious process that he calls selective inattention, which leaves out of awareness information that is contrary to one's self experience. For Sullivan, stereotypes reflect aspects of oneself that are inadequate or inappropriate. The stereotypes are personifications of these inadequacies, and they are encountered externally because of a limitation in the self. Rather than accepting that stereotypes are a shorthand for understanding the environment, Sullivan cautions about the potential to rationalize the presence of stereotypes as useful guides to understand the stranger. He does not accept this, and states that they are exactly the opposite of guides for dealing with strangers, and in fact they are handicaps for becoming familiar with strangers. Sullivan's ideas are related to the cognitive perspective about categorization. The ubiquitous nature of stereotypes and categorization promotes the question about how apparently universal conditions that are associated with prejudice can be countered.

Brewer (1999) addresses findings that suggest that often discrimination affecting outgroups can be understood in terms of preferential treatment for ingroup members, rather than animosity for the outgroup. This is dependent upon identifications with ingroups, and is aligned with Allport's and Fairbairn's contention that ingroups are primary. She acknowledges that the ultimate result is not benign and outgroups suffer in societies that are structured in such a way as to foster biased allocation of resources. These societal manifestations are associated with context-driven conditions that pertain to political power, perceived threat, and moral superiority. Brewer asks, what would allow large groups to function cooperatively and still retain important aspects that fulfill their uniqueness in relation to outgroups? This is a central component of her Optimal Distinctiveness Theory, which suggests that there is a constant need to balance uniqueness with being like the others in my group.

Another possible solution is provided by Allport (1954) in his notion of concentric loyalties in relation to superordinate groups that are ultimately more inclusive, such as from town, to nation, to shared global values. Similarly, Erikson (1985) writes about these kinds of categorical distinctions in questioning the problem of prejudice and how it might be resolved. He calls the various concentric loyalties "pseudospeciation" and advocates for an ultimate superordinate identity concept of human as a necessary antidote to prejudice. In contrast to this position, Brewer (1999) argues that conditions that highlight the need for large group interdependence can initiate intergroup conflict and hostility because mutual trust is lacking. I agree with Brewer that the solution is unlikely to be found by strictly seeking a superordinate category. Consider examples from the former Yugoslavia and Rwanda, where ethnic groups lived with a superordinate identity for many years, but the speed with which it dissolved was shocking and led to precisely the kind of violence predicted by Brewer's notion that intergroup distinctiveness is sought when the large group affiliation is too inclusive. I believe the superordinate identity solution does not provide the kind of permanent and personal identity structure necessary for people to balance needs to belong with needs to be unique by balancing autonomy with affiliation (also see Brewer, 1991). Addressing the kind of problems that emerge when identity structures are insufficient, Kelman (1999) conceptualizes a transcendent identity that can incorporate positive elements of two separate identities while maintaining the uniqueness of each identity for individuals of both groups.

There are important implications stemming from the interrelationship between stereotypes and categories. This involves the relational question that examines the role of a primary identification with an ingroup. Stereotypes are the cognitive categories that favor the ingroup by simplifying and often derogating the outgroup. However, as Allport notes, although by definition the ingroup requires an outgroup, he states that an ingroup does not need to be defined by its opposition to an outgroup. This view is challenged by social identity theory, which suggest that because people are motivated to enhance collective self-esteem, they will favor the ingroup when comparing with outgroups. Importantly, neither theory suggests that identification is the sole determinant of intergroup discrimination (Brown & Zagefka, 2005).

A similar idea that bridges several disciplines regarding the question of cooperative and satisfying intergroup relations relates to the complexity operating in many societies, and especially within individuals. This view pertains to the notion that individuals usually do not function in strict isolated dimensions, but rather operate along multiple overlapping dimensions. In a diverse society, like the United States, this is readily apparent when individuals have multiple and potentially conflicting identities. In the last chapter I will return to examine this cross-categorization (Roccas & Brewer, 2002) that more accurately depicts the human condition and offers ways to address the problem of prejudice.

CONCLUSION

The usefulness of the social object concept will need to be substantiated as clinicians think about this concept with their patients. This can take into account that interactions between people involve simultaneous evaluations of both personal traits and social group membership. This process is unavoidable and has been well documented as a categorizing brain process (Hogg &

Abrams, 1988). Collective identity tends to become salient during intergroup situations. The patient-therapist dyad can trigger collective identity in each participant, whether they are from similar or different cultures or identity groups. It is possible that not every patient will react to their cross-cultural therapist in a manner that impedes identification. Similarly, patient-therapist dyads from similar backgrounds may find that differences in terms of identity separate them and may make it difficult to form an alliance. As a patient of similar ethnic background to mine recently said to me, "you can not possibly understand me, because you obviously come from an affluent life without suffering." Although our ethnicity was similar, identity of socioeconomic class was affecting the potential of our engaging beyond our apparent large group categories. Just as important, however, is that some patients trigger unconscious and conscious reactions from therapists that may make progress difficult, or worse, rationalized as not being possible. The countertransference of the therapist involves his or her social object representations that may lead to overidentifications with collective identities that are triggered with different patients and reflect the complexity of the clinical situation.

The social object is an intrapsychic construct for representing the affiliation individuals have with large social groups. These groups become consciously known as collective identity. Collective identity tends to be highlighted during intergroup situations, and the cross-cultural patient-therapist dyad is one such context. When collective identity is salient, the social object can influence self-esteem, perception, and behavior, and individuals are perceived as group members. Indications of latent group perceptions and experiences may be surmised when material involves idealized or devalued splitting between certain individuals, such as mother and father, or between the patient and others. This is in contrast to traditional object relations that are more likely to be relevant during interpersonal situations that do not highlight intergroup differences. The social object should be considered to be separate from, but interdependent with, object representations associated with individuals. Perception of individuals as group members is unavoidable at times, and is what constitutes the salience of collective identity and the potential relevance of the social object.

Chapter Five

Attachment Theory and Prejudice

A strong component of attachment theory described by John Bowlby (1969, 1973) is the use of evolution theory and ethological evidence for understanding animal and human behavior. Although all higher primate species operate in social groups, most of Bowlby's attention is directed toward the dyad of the developing infant interacting with the mother. Still, we can glean some important implications for the role of the large group and extrapolate to the human intergroup condition. Bowlby always considers the environment in formulating his theory. Pertaining to group living, Bowlby writes that all higher primates, including humans, live in social groups that are usually stable (Bowlby, 1969). Yet, he recognizes that every species shares a habitat with a number of potentially dangerous predators, making it necessary to be protected by the group. For the most part, individuals of any species who become isolated from the group are vulnerable and can become victims.

Ainsworth (1989) suggests that attachment behavior has likely evolved through natural selection because it promotes survival. If we accept that attachment behavior is a component of human interaction, then we can examine how this relates to our attachment with large groups. Given the potential dangers in the world, we can ask if the threat leads the individual to seek the group affiliation. Or, given the relational proposition, that awareness of and affiliation with the ingroup is primary, does our affiliation with a large group provide a means of creating otherness, and then offer a place from which to perceive, and even create, danger in the environment? More than likely, neither perspective can be correct on its own, but rather we affiliate because of our nature, and the environment actually includes outgroups, some of which can become dangerous, given the epoch, and a context of competition and reliance on power. Both conditions suggest that perception of the outgroup is interdependent with the affiliation of the individual with the ingroup. Ainsworth (1989) asks if the survival value of the large group is an indication that a person must establish attachments with large groups, or if it is more accurately a function of dyadic relationships, or both. She was skeptical about the function of the large group within the attachment system, stating that by definition attachments are dyadic with specific people. This can be reexamined today. The potential usefulness of attachment theory for the study of prejudice requires that we extend the theory from its original emphasis on the relationship between the infant and caregiver to suggest something about the relationship of the individual with the large group.

This chapter will examine the role of attachment in developmentally progressive relationships, beginning with the infant and mother, the child in the family, the adult in romantic relationships, and finally the implications of attachment between the adult and the ingroup. It will become clear that attachment theory can help us understand prejudice, especially because it crosses boundaries between psychoanalysis and social psychology. Furthermore, attachment theory has an empirical literature that can ground some of our speculations about the use of relationships to compensate for vulnerability.

A central component of the attachment process in the theory involves exploration of the environment (Waters & Cummings, 2000). This is interdependent with a perception of a "secure base" that provides a safe physical and psychological space. There are two possible uses of the secure base. Originally, it was intended to be indicative of the infant's general sense of safety, but over time it came to represent the potential to explore the environment, given the security of the attachment and the proximity of the attachment figure (Rothbaum, Weisz, Pott, Miyake, & Morelli, 2000). The tendency to associate security with exploration may be an especially Western preference. In studies that examined the secure base in Japan, for example, a majority of infants were found to explore less than babies in the United States (cited in Rothbaum et al., 2000). Rather than emphasizing the impetus toward exploration and autonomy, Rothbaum et al. (2000) suggest that in non-Western (collectivist) cultures, attachment is linked with the dependence behavioral system, which is more valued in collectivist cultures. In these societies the individual values in oneself, and is valued for, an ability to accommodate, empathize with others, comply to others' wishes, and respond to social cues and norms (Rothbaum et al., 2000). As a contrast, almost half of the infants from a Northern German study were classified with an avoidant attachment pattern (Grossman, Grossman, Spangler, Suess, & Unzner, 1985), which can be interpreted as preferring to explore and as less dependent than the Japanese sample. It is clear that there are various ways to discuss these findings with terms that permeate the psychological literature and dichotomize these interpersonal styles. These dimensions have been described in terms of closeness and distance, or dependence and autonomy, or attachment and separation dynamics. Different cultures seem to prefer and facilitate more or less comfort with one dimension or the other.

Inclusion of both Eastern and Western values regarding preference and emphasis upon separation and attachment dynamics helps us to acknowledge both interdependent dimensions simultaneously. In fact, research on attachment theory may be limited by its use of self-report instruments that tend to have a linear focus. These instruments measure a movement toward separation or toward attachment, rather than considering that the individual manages both preferences in dialectic fashion. Importantly, awareness of a continuum between needs for autonomy and needs for affiliation promotes the midrange as a balanced position between these two human needs, with culture emphasizing one side or the other. Again, extremes in either direction, and in any culture, are likely to promote problems in relating. Attachment theorists studied and classified behaviors that essentially represent both of these dimensions. In support of the notion that the classifications in attachment theory are not static, research with adults often finds that people do not fit neatly into prototype categories, but rather have mixed needs (Bartholomew & Horowtiz, 1991). Initially, the particular behaviors observed in young children were interpreted to signify secure or insecure attachments with caregivers. It will become clear that the insecure dimension represents the behavioral manifestation of extremes of needs for separation or attachment, with important implications for adult behavior and, for our purposes, large group affiliation and prejudice.

CLASSIFICATIONS OF ATTACHMENT BEHAVIOR AND PREJUDICE

Ainsworth, Blehar, Waters, and Wall (1978) describe different ways that infants relate to their mothers. These patterns of attachment were assessed in a laboratory condition called the *strange situation*. This condition was designed to identify how attachment behavior in twelve-month-old infants is organized in relation to their mother when a stressful condition is introduced. It assesses individual differences in the infant's ability to use the mother as a secure base and "the attachment-exploration balance as it changes during the series of changing situations" (Bowlby, 1969, p. 336). The change that is introduced during the *strange situation* involves observing the toddler when the mother leaves the room and upon reunion. Many infants become distressed; a few do not; most are consolable, while others are inconsolable. At least four important reactions could be observed.

Ainsworth recognizes that children cannot be classified in linear fashion, and that ideally several indices for measuring attachment behavior are required. For descriptive purposes, however, initially she was able to label three patterns of attachment behavior, which she labeled B (secure), A (avoidant), and C (ambivalent) (Ainsworth et al., 1978; Bowlby, 1969). These three different patterns of behavior indicate something about the quality and security of the child's attachment with the caregiver.

Ainsworth's conspicuous placement of the secure attachment group, labeled Pattern B, is significant in that it signals the centrality of the secure attachment, with Pattern A (avoidant) and Pattern C (anxious-ambivalent) on either side. One way to interpret this is that the secure attachment pattern reflects effective management, or balance, of the avoidant and ambivalent behaviors that are considered extreme and potentially problematic. The parallel to our discussion about prejudice involves the classification of extreme behavior that reflects separation and attachment dynamics. Essentially, my interest in these patterns pertains to the influence of early development upon identity formation and large group affiliation. These early-life needs parallel later needs for autonomy and affiliation in young adults. In particular, this is vital during identity formation when young adults begin to affiliate with large groups. A basic demand at this stage of development is to maintain proportional autonomy as an individual while developing a sense of belonging to a collective. In other words, the young adult needs to belong to a larger segment of the community while not completely losing autonomy, or self. If overidentification with the large group is related to prejudice, it is suggestive of a merger between the self and large group. These early-life behavioral patterns may help shed light on the identity formation process and how overidentification is associated with prejudice.

In Ainsworth's studies, Pattern B one-year-olds show organized and goal-oriented behavior. This includes welcoming the mother back and wanting to be picked up or remain near her, and these infants are quickly calmed. Two other patterns were initially identified and represented different manifestations of an insecure attachment, but still organized behaviorally. Pattern A children are apparently disinterested and avoid their mother upon return during the *strange situation*, while the Pattern C children are ambivalent with their mother and show mixed feelings of wanting to be close and avoid their mother. Later a forth category was identified as a "disorganized" attachment, which includes children whose behavior is extreme and does not reflect either the avoidant or ambivalent patterns consistently (Main & Solomon, 1990). These children often come from homes with emotional disturbance in family members (Main & Solomon, 1990; Lyons-Ruth, 1996). Bowlby (1969) writes,

> When exploring and playing a group B infant was likely to use his mother as a secure base. Content to move away from her, he would nonetheless keep track

of her movements and from time to time gravitate back to her. The picture was that of a happy balance between exploration and attachment. None of the anxiously attached infants showed such a balance. Some tended to be passive, exploring little and/or rarely initiating contact; it was among these infants that stereotyped movements were most often observed. Others of the anxiously attached engaged in exploration, but they did so more briefly than the securely attached; and they seemed constantly concerned about mother's whereabouts. Although often eager to keep close to her and to make contact with her, doing so seemed nevertheless to give them no pleasure. (p. 338)

Attachment theory provides a framework that enables researchers and theoreticians to examine the vicissitudes of attachment and separation needs across the life span. Notably, a secure attachment style is associated with psychological health and good social adjustment in later life. This pattern of relating could be understood as the behavioral manifestation of psychological balance between needs for attachment and separation (Holmes, 1996).

Secure attachment provides the freedom to explore, and as a result of nontraumatic separations the infant gains a sense of autonomy that further facilitates the secure relationship. Therefore, attachment and separation are interdependent. Josselson (1988) describes this as autonomy growing in the context of connection, and connection growing in the context of autonomy. For Josselson (1988, 1994), attachment is not the opposite of separation-individuation, but rather is coincident with it. The immediate future of theoretical and research efforts to understand development must consider the dynamic influence of both attachment and separation as simultaneous, interdependent needs. Focusing on one, to the neglect of the other, distorts understanding of the process (Josselson, 1988). The result of work on attachment styles makes it possible to discuss healthy development in terms of an optimal balance between the vicissitudes of attachment and separation in relation to important figures. The research findings, in terms of percentage of children classified as either securely attached or insecurely attached, suggest that a small percentage, approximately 10 percent to 30 percent of children, can be identified with an insecure attachment. This may be a helpful marker of the percentage of adults who use large groups as compensatory structures for problems in self-development. Could this be an indication of the breadth of prejudice in society?

ATTACHMENT THEORY AND ADULT RELATIONSHIPS

Considerable research has been generated to examine attachment theory and the behavioral patterns that were identified in toddlers in relation to caregivers. Although there has been much speculation about the developmental implications of secure or insecure attachment, caution is usually called for when extrapolating to adulthood. Many factors can shape any child and young adult after the initial attachment pattern has been established. Bowlby (1988) writes that throughout one's life a variety of meaningful interactions may affect a person's beliefs about others' availability. Furthermore, different contexts may activate different expectations and reactions to important people in one's life. The lifespan notion has important implications about the possibility for change. This suggests that the prejudiced person can change, but, just as importantly, the nonprejudiced person can also change. Our challenge is to elaborate the conditions that may exacerbate or minimize prejudice within an individual and, on a macrosocial level, in society. For theorists and researchers of attachment theory, this involves evaluating and formulating the theory as it may inform our attachments to societal structures that provide safety. Applying the secure base concept to the family as a whole has been introduced (Byng-Hall, 1999). As development proceeds, a capacity for symbolic representation of concepts such as "my parents and family," and later large groups, influences one's experience of self and serve as the means for security (Waters & Cummings, 2000).

The relational underpinnings of attachment theory is reflected in the premise that human beings have a "propensity . . . to make strong affectional bonds to particular others" (Bowlby, 1977, p. 201). The initial bond with a caregiver is internalized and forms a template that influences perception of self and expectations of how one will be treated by others. Bowlby calls these internalized relationships *working models*. Adult relationships can modify these working models throughout one's lifetime (Ainsworth, 1982; Bowlby, 1977; 1969); however, they may also shape how adult relationships are experienced and expectations about how one will be treated.

Hazan and Shaver (1987) began to apply the concepts of attachment theory to adult romantic relationships. An important choice they made was to evaluate attachment style in adults by referring to feelings about emotional closeness, rather than the stressful reactivity evaluated in the infant in relation to the mother's leaving and returning during the experimental strange situation (Kaitz, Bar-Haim, Lehrer, and Grossman, 2004). With this change, security became a secondary consideration in adult attachment, while preference for closeness or distance began to be evaluated as indication of the attachment style. From this perspective, it is expected that the adult with a secure attachment style is comfortable with closeness and dependency, the avoidant style adult is uncomfortable with emotional closeness and dependency, and the ambivalently attached adult struggles with significant needs for emotional closeness and at the same time fears that it will not be reciprocated (Kaitz et al., 2004).

Hazan and Shaver (1987) suggest that adult romantic love reflects an attachment process, and can vary as a result of individual attachment histories. Applying the same categories that reflected the young child's relations with a caregiver, Hazan and Shaver (1987) found that securely attached adults experience their love relationships as especially happy, friendly, and trusting. Avoidantly attached lovers could be identified by fear of intimacy and emotional highs and lows, and the anxious/ambivalent lovers are obsessive about needs for reciprocation and union in their relationships, and also have emotional highs and lows. A number of studies replicated these results (Collins & Read, 1990; Feeney & Noller, 1990). For example, Mikulincer and Erev (1991) found that secure adults expect intimacy and tend to develop mutually satisfactory relationships. Adults with an avoidant style have less desire for intimacy, and yet those who maintain a relationship long enough had partners who loved them more than they expected. Finally, anxious/ambivalent adults value passionate love and want intimacy in their lives, but are disappointed by the degree they obtain, in relation to the securely attached adults. These findings suggest that a consistent formulation of attachment styles can be recognized with important adult relationships.

DEVELOPMENTAL IMPLICATIONS OF ATTACHMENT AND PREJUDICE

It appears then that attachment needs, beginning in infancy, continue to influence important relationships throughout one's life. The cognitive capacity to formulate large group distinctions is acquired by children at a very young age. One study found that children as young as three years of age acquire attitudes about ingroups and outgroups (Bar-Tal, 1996). Similarly, Aboud (2003) reports that by age five children develop racial attitudes, but appear to be primarily concerned with ingroup attachment, rather than negative attitudes toward outgroups. Findings like this indicate that large group concepts are communicated to children and are recognized very early in life. Aboud's (2003) study found that children in a homogenous school environment show a relationship between positive attitudes for the ingroup and negative attitudes toward an outgroup. This was not a consistent finding, however, with children who were in a mixed race school. Aboud (2003) tells us that we cannot assume an automatic relationship between ingroup favoritism and outgroup prejudice in simplistic fashion given the diversity of many societies. If this relationship does manifest, it is not because it is a universal process that unfolds the same way in all human beings, but rather it may involve individual and contextual differences.

The application of attachment theory to understand the individual's relationship with large groups has recently been introduced into the discussion. We can ask whether the symbolic representation of the relationship with the caregiver can extend beyond relations with individuals and incorporate meaning more akin to "my family," which is indicative of one's relation to the first social group (Fairbairn, 1952), and further along development, attachment relationships with societal large groups? One question to explore is whether the large group can function as a secure base. Social psychology has advanced a long way in promoting these ideas, as can be seen by the work on attachment theory and romantic relationships. Working from a social cognitive perspective, Smith and Henry (1996) report evidence that ingroups do become part of the self-representation. This finding is an important empirical step on the road to discussing how the large group is part of the adult's self-representation.

ATTACHMENT THEORY AND ATTACHMENT TO THE INGROUP

Leaving much of the developmental psychology of attachment theory behind, social psychologists have been mining the potential of attachment theory for discussing adult relationships and the relationship of the individual to the large group. Smith, Murphy, and Coats (1999) apply attachment theory in their examination of parallels between interpersonal relationships and attachment to large groups. These researchers elucidate some key points that must be considered further. They ask, "are attachments to relationship partners and to groups conceptually the same thing?" (p. 96). In some respects they are not, and Smith and colleagues cite findings that suggest working models of self and other can be different in different relationships (see Baldwin, Keelan, Fehr, Enns, & Koh-Rangarajoo, 1996; Brewer & Gardner, 1996; Collins & Read, 1994). They also point out that people may meet different needs through their interpersonal relationships than in their relationship with a large group. Returning to the evolutionary roots of attachment theory, however, Smith et al. (1999) suggest that dependence on groups is as fundamental as dependence on caregivers and lovers. With this in mind, they suggest that dependence and closeness with a group may be regulated by psychological systems, similar to the systems that regulate these needs with individuals, and though they may be interrelated (in my opinion), they are also independent subsystems that can influence behavior in different ways. This is an important finding that supports the discussion of the potential influence of a social object representation discussed in the last chapter. It suggests that the ingroup can influence behavior in ways that historical interpersonal relationships cannot predict.

Similar to studies of adult romantic relationships (Bartholomew & Horowitz, 1991), these researchers developed a scale that measures two independent dimensions of the individual's relationship to a large group (Smith et al., 1999). The attachment avoidance dimension measures the extent of one's desire for closeness and dependence with groups, while the attachment anxiety scale measures the extent of worry about acceptance by groups. Therefore each dimension is a continuous measure of more or less attachment preference with the group or concern about rejection by the group. This is a parallel to the two insecure classifications of Ainsworth's system, leaving out the secure attachment dimension.

As discussed above, a significant problem with measures of attachment that have been utilized by social psychologists is that they do not address the interdependence of these processes, thereby eliminating attention to the secure attachment that is more accurately represented by a balance between needs for closeness and autonomy. Measuring the midrange between separation and attachment dynamics with large groups would be especially helpful. With their instrument, Smith and colleagues (1999) report that the secure attachment to a group would be indicated if a person measures low on both dimensions of attachment avoidance and attachment anxiety. In the Smith et al. (1999) study, the avoidance scale is essentially a measure of a continuous variable of preference for separation or attachment to the large group. The dimension that measures anxiety about possible rejection by the group seems potentially useful in considering perceptions and attitudes toward outgroups, though in this study it is limited to the relationship with one's ingroup. It recalls Erikson's (1959) comment about the vengefulness of the large group toward those who are perceived to reject the ingroup (see Chapter 3). For individuals whose large group represents the self (overidentification), the perception of rejection (i.e. threat) by an outgroup could trigger the negative, retaliatory reaction by the overidentifed person. This is the person who is prejudiced toward the outgroup, regardless of context. Developmentally, they are likely to have low avoidance toward their own group and high anxiety toward the outgroup.

The notion of a secure base was reintroduced by Mikulincer and Shaver (2001) in their application of attachment theory to understand the individual in relationship with the large group. The secure base suggests that infants are less fearful of strangers when their caregiver is available (Mikulincer & Shaver, 2001). This line of research continues to extend the potential use of attachment theory from the initial emphasis on the infant–caregiver interaction. These researchers predicted, and found, that when the secure base was activated experimentally with priming techniques that present subliminal words that are presumed to be associated with a secure base schema, such as love and support, people will show less negative reactions toward outgroups. This assumes that if a secure base is available people are more open to exploration and acceptance of strangers. Mikulincer and Shaver (2001) write, "having a sense of being loved and surrounded by supporting others seems to allow people to open themselves to alternative worldviews and be more accepting of people who do not belong to their own group" (p. 110). They acknowledge that their findings need to be accepted with caution, and it should be kept in mind that studies like this collapse a group of participants, which minimizes individual differences. For example, a person who is overidentified with the ingroup may also have a high degree of "felt security" (Stroufe & Waters, 1977), but nonetheless feel negatively about the outgroup. Mikulincer and Shaver (2001) and Smith et al. (1999) attempt to assess a more nuanced individual who on one dimension is managing needs for closeness and distance with others and the ingroup, and is simultaneously managing self-experience in terms of worthiness that is played out with both the ingroup and outgroup. This rich and complex effort to evaluate the individual should consider the developmental experience of the individual, keeping in mind that context can override how one needs the group for self-worth and security. The individual who grows up with a balance between separation and attachment needs (secure attachment with a caregiver) is also more likely to have self-worth, and this individual may recapitulate this process during the identity formation stage of development.

PSYCHOANALYSIS, ADULT ATTACHMENT, AND PREJUDICE

Psychoanalysts have not made significant efforts to apply attachment theory to the study of large group affiliation, or to prejudice in particular. One exception was recently offered by Fonagy and Higgitt (2007), who discuss the role of attachment in normal and malignant prejudice in adults. They suggest that normal prejudice is activated in reaction to possible loss of a safe environment. This condition places one in a vulnerable position, which, they state, promotes an insecure working model. In an effort to reaffirm belonging, one seeks identification with the needed and similar, while exaggerating difference with the object of prejudice, or the stranger. They suggest that this is an indication of healthy functioning of the attachment system, which is why they suggest that this kind of prejudice is ubiquitous and normal. Under conditions of threat, the mentalizing function—in other words, our capacity to think about other people's thoughts, feelings, beliefs, and wishes—is unavailable. In normal prejudice this is a temporary process.

Malignant prejudice is associated with the disorganization of the attachment system and is pathological. This insecure attachment is characterized by needs for proximity to the caregiver and simultaneous paranoia (Fonagy & Higgitt, 2007). Unfortunately, Fonagy and Higgitt (2007) do not bring the large group directly into their discussion and therefore their elaboration of the dynamics of prejudice is constrained by interpersonal determinants of pathology stemming from a traumatic and difficult history. It is not clear, therefore, what constitutes a threat that leads to prejudice. They suggest that the self-system becomes disorganized as a result of failed mirroring. In an effort to recover, malignant prejudice involves use of the object (outgroup) to take on a disowned part of the self. In other words, the prejudiced person projects unacceptable parts of the self onto the other. This is essentially a classic theory of projection as the mechanism to understand why one hates a target of prejudice. The outcome is a need to see the humiliation in the target of one's unconscious aggression. Fonagy and Higgitt (2007) differentiate prognosis between these two kinds of prejudice, suggesting that contact between large groups could ameliorate normal prejudice, but change is much less likely with malignant prejudice.

RELATIONAL PSYCHOANALYSIS, ATTACHMENT, AND PREJUDICE

A relational perspective would redirect the focus from the outgroup toward the ingroup as the object to be used in the effort to recover self-coherence. This is consistent with our understanding of overidentification as a means to strengthen the self. A needed element in Fonagy and Higgitt's (2007) discussion is the role of large groups in the self-system. A person can use the large group to compensate for developmental deficits, and groups can affect the individual in new ways, just as new experiences with individuals can facilitate change. The individual knows that the large group is important as an aspect of identity. What is out of awareness is the influence of the large group in unconscious process. The greater the disturbance, or situational insecurity, the greater the influence of the social object. I think that the process of identification or overidentification with the large group is the mechanism for understanding how identity and prejudice are intertwined. Attachment theory offers one way to speak about healthy and problematic attachments, which is indicative of the identifications with caregivers, romantic relationships, and large groups.

Parens (2007) comes one step closer to the direct implications of large group affiliations in the self-system by drawing attention to the developmental influence of separation and attachment processes for identity formation and prejudice. He suggests that stranger anxiety in the infant is a forerunner to normal prejudice in adults. This normal developmental process is transformed into a destructive process when an ambivalent relationship between the infant and caregiver is established, and hate emerges toward the caregiver. For Parens (2007) understanding the urge to harm and destroy another person requires hatred. He believes that hate transforms normal prejudicial processes into a malignant process. His observations of infants lead him to reject more classical concepts, such as the death instinct to explain hatred, and acknowledge the role of ambivalence between an infant and caregiver. The role of intergroup processes and the large group in the mind of the prejudiced person is alluded to as a parallel to the relationship with a parent.

Psychoanalytic discussion of destructive prejudice could benefit by a thorough examination of the role of large groups in the identity formation process and how large groups are internalized in the minds of individuals. I agree with Parens's conclusion about the role of ambivalence in destructive reactions toward others; but again, I draw attention to the relational implications. The evolutionary dimension in this discussion suggests that it is the threat to survival of the infant, and the ingroup member, that leads to destructive reactivity toward the stranger/outgroup. The ambivalent attachment with the mother indicates that the secure base is vulnerable. This attachment style also draws attention to the intense dependence of the infant upon the caregiver. This kind of vulnerable attachment in early life can influence overidentification with the large group in early adulthood as a compensation for vulnerability, and it is heightened when societal threats are present. The secure base concept is a crucial component of the attachment theory approach to understanding prejudice in both psychoanalysis and social psychology. The secure base concept is not sufficiently utilized to show how ingroup identifications can become overidentifications in an effort to reestablish security because of either developmental or societal threat. In the next section I will connect the various strands that have been discussed and introduce a model that incorporates the central role of separation and attachment dynamics with attachment theory and prejudice.

ATTACHMENT, IDENTITY, AND PREJUDICE

Applying the concept of the secure base to the large group is, of course, an extrapolation of the needed security with a caregiver that the infant requires for survival. Reintroducing the evolutionary dimension into the model, we can formulate that the individual develops an affectional bond with the ingroup, just as with an important caregiver, and both have to do with survival. This bond facilitates safety, trust, and self-esteem. Under threatening conditions, the attachment system is activated in the young child, and the adult in relation to his or her ingroup. The quality of the secure base is signaled by the secure or insecure attachment pattern. How would attachment look in the adult in relation to the large group?

It suggests that when the context is safe, a majority of individuals may relate to outgroup members in neutral ways. Why such a hopeful estimation? There seem to be consistent findings of percentages of infants and adults with secure attachments. For example, similar to Ainsworth's studies, Lyons-Ruth (1991) reports that 60 percent to 70 percent of infants in both American and world-wide samples could be classified as securely attached. Pattern A (approximately 20 percent of sample) infants show an insecure attachment and are avoidant of their caregiver. These infants may treat a stranger in more friendly fashion than their mother. Pattern C (approximately 10 percent of sample) infants are classified with an insecure attachment and are resistant/ambivalent with their caregiver, and oscillate between seeking proximity and contact and resisting contact with the mother. From the social psychological literature Hazan and Shaver (1987) note the statistical percentages that were reported by Campos, Barrett, Lamb, Goldsmith, and Stenberg (1983), in which 62 percent of infants were classified secure, 23 percent as avoidant, and 15 percent as anxious/ambivalent. In Hazan and Shaver's initial studies with adults, they found that 56 percent of adults were classified as securely attached, 24 percent avoidant, and 20 percent anxious/ambivalent. Even with the cultural variations that were discussed earlier, these percentages are relevant when considering prejudice. First of all, it suggests that a majority of people have early-life relationships that help them balance needs for closeness with needs for autonomy. Reliance on the availability of the caregiver early in life may influence expectations of availability in adult relationships. The secure base suggests security through affiliation. The extremes reflect potential pathological affiliations, but in the service of survival. The smaller percentage of people with insecure attachments suggests that regardless of a safe context in adulthood, these individuals may need to utilize other people or large groups in compensatory ways to regulate their internal emotional needs.

We would predict that most adults, up to two-thirds, will establish supportive and gratifying affiliations with large groups (collective identity) and balance this with autonomy as an individual. Some people, however, will need to use the large group to compensate for developmental deficits. Parens's (2007) comment about the relationship between ambivalence and hatred is relevant at this point. From his research with infants, Parens (2007) concludes that, "experience-derived ambivalence in primary relationships is the most central and powerful contributor to the generation in humans of the wish to harm or destroy others" (p. 28). The insecure ambivalent group reflects significant preoccupation and need for the attachment object. These individuals may be prone to overdependence upon intimate people in their lives, and potentially to overidentification with the large group so that the large group is an effective and ongoing compensation for the vulnerability of the self. For those people who experience less differentiation between the self and other, and similarly, less differentiation between self and group, the need to keep the group/self strong reveals the underlying vulnerability. Their inner world provides an ongoing threat, and perhaps these individuals feel a constant threat as group members.

Fonagy and Higgitt (2007) speculate that the disorganized attachment style would be most associated with malignant prejudice. This is a reasonable extrapolation given the degree of pathology that is associated with this attachment style. It is important to consider the severity of the characterological pathology that emerges for each individual, rather than assuming that the entire category is likely to show malignant prejudice. The pathology of prejudice is related to, but different from, the pathology that we encounter with individuals in clinical work. For example, severe mental illness may make prejudice against other groups transient, or even impossible. As a patient declared, "I don't think about other people, because I'm in too much pain." Fonagy and Higgitt's attention to the disorganized attachment style may be relevant with some individuals with this attachment history, but in general we should be careful not to over-label so as not to see everyone in a particular category as the same.

EVOLUTION AND PREJUDICE

Incorporating an evolutionary perspective to understanding the use of the large group as a secure base suggests that behavior changes over time. Historically, the need to belong to a large group for safety may have perpetuated the prejudices that have manifested throughout history. In the current epoch, use of the large group may not be necessary in the same manner as it had been for much of history. So that today, instead of providing a secure base, the tensions that emerge between large groups actually threaten the intention of safety that such an affiliation should offer. This insecurity seems to recreate the insecure attachment of early life, but now it is within the domain of the large group.

Broadening the examination of prejudice in the individual and society, we may ask how the instinct to survive is involved. Kohut (1985) seems to draw a direct association, stating that "the basic unconscious narcissistic configu-

ration in individual existence are valid also with regard to the life of the group
. . . [and] not only account for the continuity and the cohesion of the group,
but also determine its most important actions" (pp. 206–7). Kohut's statement
is a clear endorsement of the survival instinct, which he came to believe is not
only an instinct that individuals carry, but also one that may actually become
a large group instinct that can determine action between large groups. When
the psychological boundary between the large group and the individual is reduced, then prejudice and hatred toward outgroups is an ontological concern
for the ingroup. The individual who is overidentified with the ingroup
because of developmental needs struggles with these fears in an ongoing
manner. The overidentification with the ingroup can shore up his or her self-
experience, and if environmental conditions are stable this person may be
privately prejudiced. When environmental conditions are insecure, and collective identity is salient, a majority of individuals may feel much more like
this pathological individual. At those times we cannot necessarily say that all
the people are abnormal, but we can look at the society and recognize that it
is the society that is sick. Fromm (1955/1966) has been one of the strongest
proponents of this kind of analysis.

The paradox is that the instinct for affiliation with the security-providing
ingroup may actually perpetuate ongoing threat and insecurity. However, at
this point in history as a species, intergroup cooperation would be most adaptive, and herein is the problem at the intergroup level. Ingroup overidentification (prejudice) threatens the outgroup, which leads to overidentification of
outgroup members with their own group, which can threaten the first group,
and so on in circular fashion. It becomes a vicious circle. An individual could
overidentify as an outcome of developmental insecurities, or a large segment
of society could overidentify temporarily because of a perceived or actual
threat to the society. When this occurs, the human potential for cooperation
tends to be minimized at the intergroup level.

Securely attached individuals balance autonomy as individuals with group
membership, and under threatening conditions they may experience an unavoidable temporary overidentification with the large group. The insecurely
attached adult may need to use the large group as a compensatory external
structure by overidentifying with the ingroup. This may be ongoing, regardless of environmental conditions that indicate safety or threat. This is a mechanism that is triggered by the instinct to survive. Ultimately, the relational
proposition about our nature to affiliate is a theory about survival.

Chapter Six

Society in the Consulting Room

The potential of the clinical setting to inform about prejudice and the intergroup situation requires that we evaluate relevant parallels between interpersonal dynamics and intergroup dynamics. Psychoanalysts have become experts in forging relationships with diverse individuals and in managing emotionally intensifying interpersonal climates. This experience seems especially relevant to the problem of prejudice. The intention of psychoanalytic theorists and practitioners has always been to play a positive role in people's lives. This is usually limited to the interaction between two people, the clinician and patient, in the privacy of a consultation. From time to time in the history of psychoanalysis, the ideas and experiences of the field have been applied to problems on a wider scale (Altman, 1995; Bettelheim & Janowitz, 1950; Freud, 1939, Fromm, 1941/1963; Kohut, 1985; Sullivan, 1964; Volkan, 1988; Young-Bruehl, 1996). Many significant thinkers in the history of psychoanalysis have envisioned the use of psychoanalytic knowledge to change the problematic aspects of society.

Clinical work with individuals, at times, involves a confrontation with an intractable position that the patient cannot, or does not want to, relinquish. Is it possible to learn something about prejudice by examining these moments from clinical settings? It is very difficult to decipher the conscious and unconscious influences that have been integrated throughout development, are maintained by one's context, and affect one's perception. This process tends to be perceived in a seamless manner, and differentiating between the influence of important individuals or the surrounding large groups and culture is probably impossible. For our purposes, we can begin by acknowledging that prejudice in society and psychopathology that is encountered in a clinical treatment both involve conscious and unconscious elements, and both may seem intractable.

Psychoanalysts trust that the clinical process will facilitate new experience that can be integrated into the patient's beliefs and perceptions, and a shift can occur in how one experience's oneself. To the extent that changes occur within oneself, it is likely to change relationships, increase tolerance of affect and ambiguity, as well as self-esteem, and permit less constricting use of psychological defenses, and so on, with the implication of improved satisfaction in living. No matter what the baseline is for the therapist and the patient, both are consciously and unconsciously influenced by values and beliefs of their cultures (Altman, 1995; Buechler, 2004; Rokeach, 1968). In the clinical encounter, as well as in society, values and beliefs are likely to influence one person's expectations and attitudes about another person. This can cause the former to behave in a manner that induces the latter to act in a way that confirms the former's expectation and perception (Word, Zanna, & Cooper, 1974). This has become a familiar process called the self-fulfilling prophesy (Merton, 1957; Miller & Turnbull, 1986). Clinicians are not immune from these kinds of interpersonal patterns in their work (Aviram, Brodsky, & Stanley, 2006). In general, this is a stereotyping process and is bi-directional, occurring between the patient and therapist simultaneously. If one or both individuals have negative beliefs and expectations about the other, this could lead to withdrawal and rejection by one or both individuals (Goffman, 1963). Of course, positive beliefs and expectations influence behavior and the relationship in the opposite direction.

Despite these reactions, therapists can and do work with people who are very different from themselves. Early in training, clinicians are taught to address hostility and resistance directed at them, which is expressed with questions like, "how could you understand me, were you ever abused?" or, "you have never used drugs," or, "or you're too young," or "you're a man," and so on with endless possibilities about differences. We should take notice that most psychotherapists work with a diverse group of people, from ethnicity, class, race, religion, gender, not to mention the complexity of variation that manifests in emotional health and psychological suffering. This is not to say that every therapist should be able to, or want to, work with every patient. We are acknowledging that it is possible for one person to work with another person who is quite different in terms of history, culture, emotional well-being, and countless other variables. Interestingly, this is often expected, but why should we expect this to occur in a consulting room, while at the intergroup level quite the opposite is true? We are not surprised that positive working alliances do not develop, and may even be hostile, between certain large groups or individuals acting as members of various large groups. What makes differences so influential between certain ingroups and outgroups, and how do psychotherapists seem able to surmount this potential obstacle?

THE CLINICAL ENCOUNTER

Social psychology may offer one way to begin to understand differences between the interpersonal context of psychotherapy and the dynamics that emerge between large groups in society. Luhtanen and Crocker (1992) draw our attention to context as an identity-triggering variable. In an interpersonal context, typical of psychotherapy, the characteristics of each individual become salient. This reflects traits and personal attributes, such as smart, tall, friendly, or anxious. Perhaps this partly explains how, in the two-person context of a psychotherapy session, people manage to establish a rapport with each other even when they may be quite different from one another in terms of large group memberships. In other words, they ultimately relate to one another as individuals, rather than as members of different large groups.

From a psychoanalytic perspective, Kohut (1985) stresses that there are important differences between large group processes and individual dynamics that are encountered in the dyadic context of psychoanalysis. He focuses on the transferences that become oriented toward one person and have a chance to be worked through. His attention, however, is on transferences that are based on historical individuals, without acknowledging that how one has incorporated the large group may influence the transference, and that large group dynamics may play out between two individuals. Kohut's perspective is not uncommon for clinicians who are oriented toward, and expert with, individual and interpersonal dynamics. Although he draws attention to the possibility of a group self as an analogy to the individual self, he seems to place this group self outside the mind of the individual—something that has a life of its own out in the world, rather than also considering how the group self may be internalized within the individual.

Volkan (2002), too, suggests that extrapolation from individual psychotherapy to large group dynamics has its limits. Nonetheless, it is relevant, he writes, to consider the parallels between the clinician helping to interpret the influences of childhood traumas on a patient, and likewise the policymaker identifying shared historical traumas between two large groups that keeps them bound to one another in constant tension. Volkan writes that clinical work with individuals permits the analyst to tolerate negative affect projected onto the analyst. The safety of the therapeutic space helps the analyst to tolerate this affect, and through the mutual containment of this affect the patient develops broadened awareness of himself and others. In contrast, political strategies necessary in the large group context cannot rely on this kind of safe structure. Instead, change in the large group domain is accompanied by identity confusion, which, Volkan writes, may set in motion dangerous social or political movements. He suggests that rather than integration and development of a cohesive self-representation, which is the objective for individual work, coexistence between two large groups requires maintenance of a psychological and political border between two opposing large group identities (Volkan, 2002). These psychological borders, however, ultimately require attention in the effort to repair and establish new relations between large groups.

Let us return to the clinical setting. The initial encounter between a patient and a therapist can evoke both conscious and unconscious elements of identity for both participants. These reactions may become most evident in cross-cultural patient-therapist dyads, as both cannot help but be aware of being in the presence of a member from a different identity group. Comas-Diaz and Jacobsen (1987) stress the importance of discussing cultural differences between individuals as critical to favorable outcome in psychotherapy. Similarly, Akhtar (2006) and Altman (2006) speak of the necessity of attending to the choice that has been made by the patient to work with a particular analyst, so that unconscious aspects of identity are brought to light. If some degree of identification with a therapist is necessary (Weiner, 1982), the extent to which differences and similarities associated with identity interfere or aid in this process requires attention.

At the beginning of a treatment both the analyst and patient are immediately aware of each other's large group identity. From the social psychological perspective, we could say that collective identity is temporarily highlighted. For example, the therapist is a woman, she is Caucasian, and her last name is such and such, which may mean she is Christian, and maybe ethnically Italian. These early assessments play a role in the mind of the patient and have some bearing on collective identity. To the extent that collective identity matters to the patient (or the analyst), large group identifications could influence how the patient and therapist interact with each other. It would seem that these large group perceptions, or social object transferences (see chapter 4), influence perception and reaction in unique ways, and in addition to transferences that develop with the analyst and that pertain more directly to individuals from the patient's history. We may even say that the social object transference is interwoven with the transference associated with traditional object relations (individuals); for how can we differentiate ourselves from the large groups in which we are members? The degree of importance that collective identity has in our experience may give us one way to attend to this process in a clinical setting.

It matters how two people overcome this potential area of divergence, which would make the treatment difficult or even impossible to begin. We know that many treatments do not get off the ground and patients leave after one, or a few, sessions. It is usually not possible to assess whether the choice to leave psychotherapy is related to an assessment on the part of the patient that the clinician is too different from themselves, in terms of the categories of large group identity that we are discussing. Just as important is our ability to attend to the therapist's behavior and the manifestation of the self-fulfilling prophecy.

THE SUBTLE EFFECT OF STIGMA

Diagnosis is another form of categorizing and may unconsciously influence subtle rejecting comments and behaviors on the part of the therapist. For example, certain diagnoses become stigmatized in society and by practitioners. A stigma is the perception of a negative attribute that becomes associated with global devaluation of the person (Katz, 1981). Goffman (1963) characterizes stigma as an attribute that is discrediting. Those who are stigmatized are diminished in the minds of those perceiving the negative attribute. An important feature of Goffman's analysis is that persons perceiving the stigma voluntarily distance themselves from those who are stigmatized. We know that mental illness is one of the most stigmatized conditions in the United States, if not the world (Westbrook, Legge, & Pennay, 1993). Clinicians are not immune from influence of the surrounding culture, including the culture that has developed among psychotherapists. Negative expectations or attitudes toward certain categories of diagnosis can initiate these distancing behaviors (Aviram, Brodsky, & Stanley, 2006). The manifestation of these patterns in the clinical setting attests to how difficult it may be to recognize and counter prejudiced perceptions and behaviors in an uncontrolled setting such as society-at-large.

UNCONSCIOUS PREJUDICE

In nonclinical settings, nonconscious prejudice has been researched by social psychologists and called aversive racism. Gaertner and Dovidio (1986), and Dovidio, Kawakami, and Gaertner (2000), suggest that this form of prejudice can manifest in many people who sincerely support egalitarian principles and consciously believe they behave in nonprejudiced fashion. Unconsciously though, they may have negative feelings about historically disadvantaged groups that influences their choices in certain contexts. Prejudice of this sort should not be limited to powerful or majority group members, and we should consider prejudice that is out of awareness that affects relations between minority groups, and also within groups. These researchers believe that aversive racism is in part a function of the categorizing brain process, along with internalization of racially biased values and beliefs. They suggest that the conflict between consciously held egalitarian views and unconscious negative feelings creates ambivalence, which may be expressed in subtle, indirect, and rationalized ways. They suggest that discrimination will occur in contexts that do not make obvious what constitutes appropriate or inappropriate behavior, or when a negative response can be justified on factors other than race. Gaertner and Dovidio (1986) are clear that prejudice and discrimination persist in society; however, today it is subtler, indirect, and less overtly negative than in the past. Given the strictures of contemporary society, significant psychological maneuvers are enacted to promote a nonprejudiced self-image.

Ambivalent feelings develop in relation to the tension between a positive view of oneself as an ingroup member, in relation to an outgroup, about which negative feelings have seeped into unconscious process. This would be an unavoidable outcome of the integration of culture, which includes both positive and negative values regarding both ingroups and outgroups. We can ask whether majority group members are less aware of this process, as alluded to by Dovidio and colleagues, than minority group members. In a discussion with a group of psychology interns, I made reference to a phrase Edgar Levinson uses, "fish are the last to know about water," to describe transference experiences. I was using this phrase to refer to the subtle influence of culture. A perceptive intern pointed out that some fish might know more about water than other fish if they jump out of it. The intern's comment reminds us that those of us who do not feel accepted in a given society may be acutely aware of the surrounding culture in that we may actually be on the outside, like the jumping fish. It begs the question, to what extent is collective identity salient for minority group members as they navigate a society in which they may feel like outsiders? If it is so, then is it associated with more consciousness about prejudiced thoughts and feelings that are related to collective identity, and which may be unconscious for majority group members? Psychoanalysts might consider these processes in terms of defense mechanisms. Prejudice that is unconscious and expressed under ambiguous conditions would involve denial and rationalization to protect the self.

INTEGRATED THREAT AND TERROR THEORY

There are certain large group conditions that seem especially relevant for attention in the clinical setting. Integrated Threat Theory (Stephan and Renfro,

2003) and Terror Management Theory (Pyszczynski, Solomon, and Green-berg, 2003) are two social cognitive perspectives that address intergroup dynamics by incorporating the very human fear of death. Stephan and Renfro (2003) suggest that prejudice and threat are closely linked. In their theory they identify four types of threat that they say cause prejudice. They classify threats into realistic group threats, symbolic group threats, realistic individual threats, and symbolic individual threats. The first are realistic threats that include any threat that can have an impact on the welfare of the ingroup's political or economic power. This could involve competition for limited resources, as realistic conflict theory predicts (LeVine & Campbell, 1972), but is broader to allow for any kind of tangible threat. Symbolic group threats pose danger to the ingroup's value system, or belief system. These threats can be intangible and can cause prejudice by drawing attention to differences in cultures. Realistic individual threats occur during intergroup contact. Anxiety stems from the fear of being harmed, and symbolic individual threat is about the risk of embarrassment when interacting with outgroups, or concern about negative evaluation by outgroup members and possible negative evaluations by ingroup members. Finally, stereotypes can lead to either group-level or individual-level threat, depending on the context and the perceiver, and can lead to anticipation that outgroups will be hostile. Negative contact with outgroup members could lead to feeling threatened in an ongoing way, and, similarly, status disparities will lead to intergroup threat as both ingroups and outgroups struggle with concerns about power. Stephan and Renfro (2003) believe that greater levels of identification with an ingroup are associated with more susceptibility to feeling threatened by outgroups.

Pyszczynski, Solomon, and Greenberg (2003) propose a similar formulation that they call *terror management*. They suggest that in order to manage the fear of death, people cling to identity structures, and greater fear leads to greater adherence to our identity structures. Both perspectives indicate that the stronger that one is identified with the large group, the more likelihood that prejudice will arise toward the threatening outsider. Strenger (2007) suggests that our instinct to survive as individuals, and by extension large groups, perpetuates the intense clinging to ideological frameworks as a way to ward off the realistic threats that intergroup conditions trigger.

OVERCOMING DIFFERENCE

When two people are working well together in a psychotherapeutic context, and on the surface they are very different from each other, we can assume that they have made a connection that transcends these categories of distinction, and that they recognize their common humanity. Perhaps the one-on-one context facilitates a capacity for empathy that recognizes a shared human experience. It eliminates the pseudospeciation that Erikson (1956) was so condemning of, allowing both therapist and patient to engage in a collaborative process of mutual responsibility. The clinical context, at least for individual therapy, is an interpersonal context that may allow many people to overcome concerns about collective identity and safety in relation to the therapist.

Furthermore, it is not common for a patient to declare that the therapeutic task is to understand how prejudice is interfering in his or her life. This is why it is very difficult to gauge the frequency with which issues of large group prejudice are discussed during psychotherapy (Sullaway & Dunbar, 1996). It is, however, an emerging area in the literature, and this may lead to clarification and more thorough attention to the therapeutic relevance of these dynamics. Clearly, some clinicians are addressing the implications and impact of prejudice on their patients, though many questions remain. For example, do these issues emerge more frequently with minority therapists who work with patients of similar or dissimilar ethnicity, race, gender, or variation in religious orthodoxy, etc. (Akhtar, 1999; Aronson, 2007; Dalal, 2002; Leary, 2000; Layton, 2006)? Are Caucasian therapists more or less likely to consider this as a topic in their work (Altman, 2006)? How do cross-cultural patient-therapist dyads address these differences (Altman, 1995; Akhtar, 2006; Bonovitz, in press; Hamer, 2006)? Just as important to consider is how apparent similarity may close off areas for consideration in therapy that pertains to collective identity with an assumption that certain things are understood (Altman, 2006). The clinical encounter shows us that it is possible for two people who come from very different life circumstances, and who harbor their own prejudices, to also have a supportive, productive, and intimate working relationship.

UBIQUITOUS PREJUDICE OR INDIVIDUAL PATHOLOGY

In popular and professional culture, certain prejudices have become linked with mental illness. For example, xenophobia, homophobia, or Islamophobia suggest something about the fear of the prejudiced person. These formulations of fear seem directly related to threat theory or terror management theory, discussed above. These individuals are phobic to the point of irrational fears about foreigners, homosexuals, or Muslims, but can we say that prejudice is a mental illness? This fear-based attention to prejudice may have its developmental roots in the stranger anxiety of the infant. Parens (2007) examined the interrelationship between separation anxiety and stranger anxiety that was described by Spitz (1965). His observational research found that during crucial periods in early development, as the attachment process is stabilizing, infants are susceptible to intensified anxiety when attachment to the caregiving figure is threatened. Parens believes that stranger anxiety is a key developmental parallel to xenophobia in adulthood. He offers an important relational interpretation about stranger anxiety, however, by speculating that stranger anxiety may redirect the infant toward the caregiver. This suggests that fear of the stranger is a reaction to the insecurity of the attachment one has with the caregiver. Perhaps we can say that the adult xenophobe is fearful, but not necessarily strictly fearing the outgroup, as a phobia would suggest. Instead, the fear pertains to security of the relationship with the ingroup, indicating the need to have a secure ingroup for one's personal survival. This redirects attention to the affiliation with the ingroup, rather than prejudice being about the fear of an outgroup. The adult who experiences the large group and self as interchangeable (overidentification with the ingroup) may become quite anxious if the attachment with the large group is threatened by, for example, competition for resources with outgroups or threat to the values of the ingroup. Keep in mind that for these individuals there is no differentiation between the ingroup and the self.

The identity formation process in early adulthood involves one's affiliation with large groups. We have discussed how in adolescence this process is akin to a temporary overidentification with the ingroup and how those overidentifications can ultimately lead to discrimination against certain outgroup members. It is also possible that certain individuals use the large group to compensate for developmental deficits in their experience of self beyond adolescence. An overidentification with large groups can also occur to large segments of society during periods of environmental stress that make collective identity salient but temporary. These experiences are so common that our familiarity with different manifestations of prejudice, both in its developmental form and when it seems to affect many people at the same time, can lead us to make the common distinction that has been referred to as pathological prejudice versus normal prejudice. This is basically the difference in focus between psychoanalysis and social psychological approaches to the study of prejudice. Akhtar (2007) reminds us, though, that just because prejudice may be pervasive as a human condition, we should not accept it as any less pathological than the extreme hatred of a disturbed individual.

The distinction between pathological and normal processes of prejudice is becoming an important consideration for clinical researchers, as well as the general public. For example, *The Washington Post* (Vedantam, 2005) published a story in which some mental health practitioners supported the creation of a diagnostic category that pathologizes extreme bias. Once again, the criteria for defining prejudice of this sort is extreme fear and worry about outgroups, similar to a specific phobia. These individuals may rearrange their lives so as to avoid the feared outgroup member. From this perspective, the goals of treatment are the reduction of symptoms, which lends itself well to defining prejudice as a fear-based problem. The criteria is the negative reaction to the outgroup, which could involve fear and anxiety, as well as negative consequences to the prejudiced person resulting from societal disapproval of overt prejudice. Unfortunately, this focus misdirects attention to the outgroup, rather than considering the etiological importance of the ingroup and attending to factors that disturb that affiliation.

Sullaway and Dunbar (1996) report on three cases in which race and ethnic prejudice became a clinical focus during a cognitive behavioral psychotherapy. These researchers concede that chronic prejudice cannot be conceived of as one diagnostic category. They distinguish between transient prejudice, which is triggered by situational conditions, and chronic and pathological prejudice, which they attribute to longstanding personality disorders. They identify that chronic or pathological prejudice is characterized by a rigid belief system about the outgroup, difficulty controlling an impulse to negatively react to outgroup members, and interpersonal difficulties that stem from these cognitive and reactive problems. The transient type of prejudice may begin following a traumatic event that involves members of different outgroups, while no such event is necessary for the chronically prejudiced person. Either form of prejudice should also be influenced by the conditions of a particular society, which may make security concerns with specific outgroups more salient. This could involve threats from the outside, such as an enemy, or internal to the society, such as economic instability. In the United States both of these conditions threaten the population at various times, and we see that political policies and a popular outcry for immigration reform and border restrictions can emerge. Together they are supposed to address the external threat of terrorism, as well as the internal threat of economic competition.

For some people prejudicial reactions are ego-syntonic and the individual does not have a subjective feeling that there is anything wrong with his or her prejudice. These individuals would not meet criteria for a phobia disorder anyway, given that the subjective experience is not disturbing for these people. Other individuals report a prejudice about certain outgroups following some kind of negative interaction with members of that group, and they may feel quite distressed by their reactions. These conditions need to be differentiated from cultural manifestations of prejudice or cases in which the person hates outgroups without any apparent environmental or cultural influences. A psychoanalytic approach does not discount symptom relief, but it expands the emphasis of the psychotherapy to incorporate sociological, developmental, and characterological implications. The cases presented by Sullaway and

Dunbar (1996) suggest that longstanding characterological conditions in which prejudice toward outgroups is a factor are less likely to change during a cognitive behavioral treatment that is not attentive to the characterological issues that underlie the prejudice. I want to acknowledge that I favor a psychoanalytic approach to treatment without the absolute conviction that my approach is the best one. It is very difficult to differentiate preferences from biases and prejudices, and yet each of these positions requires that one avoid self-righteous absolute truth, by balancing conviction with acceptance of difference, even for psychotherapeutic approaches.

On one hand, prejudice is an unavoidable expression of human preference and reactivity, and in a certain context or epoch many people may have an extreme negative reaction toward certain outgroups. Therefore it is not useful to have a diagnostic category that pathologizes a behavior that is practically universal. On the other hand, some individuals are extreme in this behavior and act out hostility and aggression in a way that is clearly idiosyncratic and a manifestation of a pathological process. Differences between "benign" and "malignant" prejudice help to focus attention on both the ubiquitous nature of prejudice and also on the unique problematic behavior of certain individuals. It may be a more accurate effort to identify differences in etiological processes that intensify prejudice in either one individual or a group of people. Prejudice may involve a range of psychological processes, in many cases not pathological, while others can include delusional and anxiety disorders and personality variables. Both conditions are influenced by developmental conditions as well as environmental and contextual considerations.

A psychoanalytic treatment could conceptualize a process that addresses the relevance of separation and attachment processes in relation to individuals in the person's life and history, as well as the implications for identity formation as it pertains to large group affiliations. Symptom relief is an important criterion, and, in cases that prejudice is reactive to specific events or temporary environmental conditions, this is likely to abate more quickly. In contrast, promoting lasting change with individuals who have entrenched prejudices is likely to involve characterological problems that are indicative of underlying threats to the survival of the self. There is no formula for discussing these dynamics with any given patient. It is likely, however, that involvement in a thriving psychoanalysis will help one feel safer in the world in general.

BELIEFS AND STEREOTYPES

Prejudice involves both an attitude of favor or disfavor and an overgeneralized, and therefore erroneous, belief (Allport, 1954). Typically, when an exaggerated belief is associated with a category, it is called a stereotype. Allport clarifies that the stereotype is not identical with the category, but, as he puts it, "it is a fixed idea that accompanies the category" (p. 187). The stereotype serves to simplify the category, which is directly related to the defense mechanisms to be discussed in the next section. Allport knew quite well that the defense mechanism of rationalization is effective in accommodating a belief to an attitude. Although beliefs can be challenged with examples to the contrary, the prejudiced person tends to find exceptions or reasons to maintain the prejudice. Can we say then, that these extreme beliefs are more akin to delusions? An extreme example will illustrate the fundamental elements of this process, and yet the extraordinary circumstances to be described do not make the result alien to any of us.

Milton Rokeach's (1964) *The Three Christs of Ypsilanti* demonstrates how essential identity is for survival of the individual psyche, and the extent to which people will go to protect their self-concept. Rokeach examines how core beliefs about identity might be attenuated when information is presented that challenges these beliefs. He developed a relationship with three men suffering with a psychotic disorder and who were institutionalized at the Ypsilanti State Hospital in Michigan. Each of the three men believed that he was the Son of God. When confronted with two additional men who believed the same thing, Rokeach wanted to see how they would accommodate this condition, hoping that they would abandon their delusion. At that time, these men had been truly institutionalized, two for about twenty years and one for approximately five years. As we might expect, the youngest man, with the least time at the hospital, improved the most, but still in a limited way. He tried to maintain a coherent narrative about his life as he was faced with obvious challenges to his belief system. The other two men, ultimately, did not even try to present a logical explanation about themselves. In order to maintain some semblance of self-coherence they desperately utilized defenses of denial and rationalization extensively in order to diminish the authenticity of the other two "false" messiahs. This is a fascinating account of the extent to which men will go in order to survive. The longstanding nature of their delusions suggests that underlying needs to establish and hold onto a grandiose character could not be overcome by simply presenting evidence to the contrary. We can say that delusions are extreme versions of prejudice in the realm of erroneous beliefs. Rokeach's study of three men who are desperately seeking to ward off annihilation anxiety gives some indication of the desperation and intensity of the need to hold on to an identity. Rokeach concludes his book with an overly optimistic note. He writes, we have learned that even when a summit of three is composed of paranoid men, deadlocked over the ultimate in human contradiction, they prefer to seek ways to live with one another in peace rather than destroy one another. (p. 332)

I refer to this comment as optimistic because I am skeptical of whether, in an unstructured context that challenges intergroup relations, men will actually seek ways to live with one another in peace. We have countless examples of the destructiveness that is unleashed when threats to identity arise and when authority is not imposed to contain hostile and destructive impulses. When beliefs are intertwined with emotion that signals that survival is at stake, and survival was exactly what was at stake for the three Christs, we can anticipate that extreme measures will be engaged. The safe and structured context of the hospital, and the authority of the staff, likely protected these men from eliminating the threat to their identity with destructive force. In contrast, identity groups who are no longer protected by the authority of a government may be at risk of being attacked because of their perceived threat to a different large group identity. We have seen this repeatedly, and there is no shortage of examples, which I choose not to provide so as to not highlight some over others. Perhaps we can say that when prejudice turns to hatred and the context is such that destruction is a potential outlet, a kind of societal psychosis is occurring.

DEFENSES AND HATE

Prejudice becomes a virulent destructive process because of emotions. When prejudice changes from belief to hatred, a transformation has taken place that is important to understand. We must ask, what has become so unbearable? The answer must be that life itself is at stake. *The Three Christs of Ypsilanti* demonstrates that human beings will use extreme measures to maintain identity. In the example of the three Christs we can see the defensive use of massive denial, rationalization, and splitting to protect an idealized and powerful self-structure. It is an example of the extreme need to avoid knowing contradictions within one's own self-concept by eliminating the authenticity of the other. Could we not surmise that the annihilation anxiety that these men faced demanded such extreme psychological measures? It calls our attention to the possibility that this can occur in nonpsychotic individuals whose identity is threatened or in large groups that feel a similar threat.

The extent to which prejudice can be so destructive must mean that the most serious consequences may occur. It must indicate that survival is at risk, signaled by annihilation anxiety that is associated with large group identity (see chapter 7). Similar to the three Christs, whose existence was dependent upon the maintenance of their individual identities, when extreme prejudice is evident in the nonpsychotic individual we know that his or her identity is intertwined with the existence of the large group. At those times there is no differentiation between the self and large group, so that action for the self and for the group cannot be distinguished. If one is acting to protect the group, one is really acting to protect the self. There is a dialectic process that operates and facilitates the survival of both the individual and the large group simultaneously.

The negative beliefs about the other that are central to the definition of prejudice must include feelings ranging from dislike to hate, and discomfort to fear. As we know, sometimes these feelings are a result of an actual frightening, shaming, or threatening experience that involves the outgroup. At other times one's family or society socially sanctions them. Context may make a difference as to the extent to which action is initiated, as well as the kind of action. Of particular interest are the developmental processes that influence overidentification with the large group. Whatever the circumstances, these negative beliefs and feelings will always be justified, rationalized, and usually accepted as a truth if identity is at stake.

Psychoanalytic theory most often relies on projection as the defense mechanism that neatly explains how prejudice can manifest. The theory suggests that projection eliminates the prejudiced person's own unbearable impulses by perceiving them in an outgroup, who is then hated and attacked for apparently possessing the unacceptable impulses. Although projection is a longstanding explanation of the way internal processes are externalized, I am hesitant to accept this defensive process as an explanation of prejudice. It focuses on the target of prejudice as the perceived bad object, rather than maintaining the focus on the relationship of the individual with the ingroup as the central mechanism to understand prejudice. Instead, the defense mechanism of splitting, which involves idealization of the ingroup and devaluation of the outgroup, seems more functional and parsimonious. This defense mechanism can be integrated with the social identity theory proposition that people try to maintain a positive view of the ingroup in an effort to enhance self-esteem and security. Simultaneously, there is an automatic effort to maximize difference with the outgroup, while maximizing homogeneity with other ingroup members. Overidentification with the ingroup and the defensive use of massive denial, rationalization, and splitting must reflect a compensation in an effort to contain the annihilation anxiety that becomes associated with the outgroup.

These defense mechanisms assist in the transformation of negative belief to hatred of the outgroup. Defenses maintain adherence to perceptions of outgroups as dangerous and bad, and thereby justify the hatred in the mind of the prejudiced person. Fromm (1947/1966) writes that one hates whatever threatens life. He states that this takes form as rational hate for most people and is reactive to the threatening conditions of the environment. Fromm also accounted for a second kind of hatred that is characterologically determined and is similarly reactive to the environment, but it tends to be pervasive and ultimately irrational. Fromm's comments support the proposition that both forms of hatred are compensations for an underlying threat that the person seeks to eliminate and, in the case of prejudice, finds an outlet for in the form of outgroups. The hatred directed at the outgroup provides relief and facilitates self-coherence, ultimately maintaining the overidentification with the ingroup. This is paradoxical in that it leaves one vulnerable because the self and large group are now indistinguishable, and survival of one is dependent on the other. This is an inherently vulnerable situation for the individual.

ATTENDING TO HATE

At a conference on prejudice (2006), someone asked Salman Akhtar a question about how to treat prejudice. What I remember of his answer is, "with love, of course." Similarly, Suttie (1935/1988) writes that in a state in which there is no differentiation between self and other, both love and anger are directed toward others. For Suttie, hate is intensified when separation from the needed object is threatened, and it is intended to preserve the self. Suttie's work is one of the original relational expositions, and as it relates to the topic at hand, we see how the primary effort is the restoration of the affiliation with the ingroup for one's survival. The hatred associated with prejudice toward the outgroup is especially likely when there is no differentiation between the self and the ingroup. For Suttie, the "modus operandi" of treatment is to overcome hate with love, to master anxiety, and to mitigate the severity of the super-ego.

As clinicians, psychoanalysts can attend to the underlying motivations and needs that can sustain prejudice toward outgroups. This is less likely to be a direct inquiry of treatment; rather it necessitates a consideration of the internal and external conditions that prohibit a capacity to feel secure in one's self-love and ability to direct that potential toward important others. We return to the basic conditions for identity development as the more likely focus of an ongoing psychotherapy. At the heart of the matter is the notion of optimal balance between autonomy and affiliation. This is akin to Brewer's (1991) work on optimal distinctiveness. The emphasis during individual psychotherapy or psychoanalysis is on how the person manages his or her experience of self in relation to others. The implication is that the outcome of that process will also be indicative of one's relationship with large groups.

Recall Blatt's (1990) contention about the interrelationship between self-definition and satisfying interpersonal relationships, and that extremes dichotomize these mutually reinforcing needs. Regardless of the dimension emphasized by the person's character and the implications for interpersonal relating, individuals will also utilize the large group in an effort to protect and enhance the self or the needed relationships in their lives. Both efforts are in the service of survival, and therefore the potential to overidentify with the large group may occur. We are speaking here strictly in terms of internal motivations and are leaving environmental influences aside for the time being. The large group will become a structure from which self-esteem enhancement, and especially security, will be sought.

ATTENDING TO HUMILIATION

So far this analysis of the process of changing prejudice through individual psychotherapy is in a vacuum. Both the therapist and the patient are functioning within a society and subgroups that interrelate in that society. The society itself is functioning within an interactive field with other societies. Putting aside characterological implications for prejudice, some prejudice is a result of actual occurrences between large groups. This can be in reaction to one episode with an individual from an outgroup, or it may be an ongoing problem between large groups. Both conditions are likely to represent power relations (Dalal, 2002), where one person or group experiences humiliation associated with weakness that has been exposed. Lewis (1971) writes that if a person is humiliated, hostility is often the reaction engaged toward the source of the humiliation. O'Leary and Watson (1995) clarify how in contrast to shame, the humiliated person's attention is diverted from his or her own deficiencies toward the other person's role in exposing them. This is a very important distinction between shame and humiliation. The experience of shame may lead the person to want to hide and withdraw because the focus is on the person's own negative attributes (or whatever he or she perceives as such). Whereas humiliation calls attention to the other person's power and aggression, and the emphasis is on the other's willful desire, even sadistic pleasure, in belittling the humiliated person (O'Leary & Watson, 1995).

We can see how the experience of humiliation between large groups can preoccupy individuals whose collective identity is salient and who see the outgroup as an evil sadistic oppressor. O'Leary and Watson (1995) suggest that humiliation can function as a defense against shame by directing attention from self-blame to blaming the other. If this is the case, we can extend our understanding of prejudice by incorporating the function of humiliation.

The extent to which collective identity is salient and the degree to which identification between the self and ingroup is present suggest that as interactions
between ingroups and outgroups take place, the less powerful person/group
can convert the experience of being hated into hatred of the more powerful
oppressing and denigrating outgroup. We see in this example how we can lose
the arbitrary classification of the ingroup's prejudice toward the outgroup.
Each group is both the ingroup and outgroup simultaneously.

CONCLUSIONS FOR THE CLINICAL SETTING

The normal processes that social psychologists study can affect any and all
individuals at various times, and they are especially dependent upon the context. The safety of the consulting room allows both the therapist and the patient to disarm and relate to one another as human beings who share the experience of living. Beyond that, they struggle to develop an intimacy that
transcends the actual moments that they spend together and, ultimately, to
create something together that is greater than the sum of the sessions. Forty-
five minutes plus forty-five minutes and so on for as many as they agree to
pursue hopefully adds up to something that cannot be explained by the time
they spent together. To the extent that the objectives that were discussed
above could be facilitated, it is an empirical question as to whether the contextual conditions that would cause most human beings to think of themselves
more as group members than as individuals could be diminished in the psychotherapy setting. Will the individual who has developed a balance between
autonomy and affiliation forget that "we are all more simply human than otherwise," when the environment highlights collective identity? Or is forgetting
also "just as simply human," and the idealized optimal balance does not protect us from the possibility of prejudice? I do not doubt that when life is
threatened individuals will react in extreme ways. Psychoanalysts attend to
the threats to individual psyches, while social psychologists attend to the
threats that wax and wane upon large groups. Under both conditions the relationship of the individual to the large group is paramount. Both fields study
the conditions that threaten the capacity of the individual to maintain a coherent self-concept. The role that threat plays is paradoxical in that the individual gives up personal autonomy by merging with the large group in order
to ward off annihilation anxiety and maintain or achieve self-coherence. At
those moments, the social object has more influence because threats elicit unconscious strategies for survival.

For many this is a temporary consequence, and as the context shifts they
regain balance with their autonomy. Still, those phases carry longer-term

consequences for the individual who finds that he or she is capable of destructive acts upon other human beings that, under different circumstances, they would not imagine themselves capable of. For others, this merger with the large group is an ongoing and necessary capitulation. This individual is seeking to survive by grasping the power of the idealized group to make up for the annihilation anxiety that has been developmentally shaped. Another paradox is that this kind of compensation accounts for the potential of this troubled individual to function quite well with members of his or her ingroup. This is perhaps one reason that prejudice is so much out of awareness, in that it is too much of a contrast to know that one is a good father and simultaneously a racist. The intergenerational implications are also interesting. A child raised by a parent who is overidentified with his or her ingroup may receive parenting that is stable and consistent, promoting the optimal balance between separation and attachment processes that affect character development and large group affiliations. This child will grow up with different needs associated with collective identity than those that the parent had when he or she utilized the large group for self-coherence, self-esteem, and security.

Our capacity to attend to the relational underpinnings of prejudice as a defense against annihilation anxiety and a compensation to protect the self by overidentifying with the ingroup promotes a perspective on prejudice in which love does play a role. This requires our emphasis on early-life environments that lead to insecure attachments and thereby overdependence upon the caregiver and the parallel conditions that lead to overidentification with large groups. If we accept that overidentification with an ingroup is a central mechanism for prejudice, then facilitating new strategies that would enhance personal safety, psychically and physically, and one's optimal balance between personal autonomy and belonging may minimize the conditions that lead to such compensation.

Chapter Seven

The Relational Origins of Prejudice

The ingroup has been missing from the psychoanalytic study of prejudice. Reorienting the emphasis of study toward the fundamental relevance of our affiliative nature draws attention to the interrelationship of the prejudiced person with his or her ingroup. Our effort to examine the association between the self and ingroup will provide basic information needed to understand how and why problems in relating to the outgroup develop. This is a corollary to clinical evidence that early-life relationships with caregivers can support or debilitate the quality of subsequent interpersonal relationships. The focus here is on understanding that the cause of prejudice stems from an aberration of the self/ingroup boundary. It is clear that prejudice is a human condition that reflects normal processes and exposes pathological conditions. Although prejudice is an ever-present problem between human social groups, this should not discourage us from seeking to understand and minimize the destructive manifestation of this condition. In fact, evolution of our species and evolution of societal structures offers us a unique opportunity to reconsider the inevitable nature of prejudice.

Prejudice reflects a process of opposition toward people who are considered to be outsiders in some manner. This familiar perspective about certain people who are outsiders, and recognition of those who are insiders, has influenced world history in many ways, over many epochs. The behavior seems to have an evolutionary purpose that orients us to conditions that interact with our basic instinct to survive. This is perhaps at the heart of explaining why the betrayal of a traitor or a spy is so feared and hated. It disorients our capacity to trust that we are secure when a person who has been "one of us" threatens the very core of our need to rely on members of the ingroup that protects us.

Context and environmental conditions influence our perceptions of self and other by affecting the degree of importance placed on evaluations of ingroup or outgroup status. The most significant environmental condition that controls our perception in this way is war. During wartime, entire societies are functioning as ingroups that threaten, and simultaneously are threatened by, the outgroup. There is an automatic insecurity aroused when we encounter members of outgroups during periods of tension at the intergroup level. This accounts for the possibility of internment camps that imprison citizens of a country who have a bicultural identity once part of their identity is labeled "enemy." Groups in conflict do not perceive their enemy in personal terms. In other words, each individual member is disidentified (Moss, 2003), and negative expectations about the outgroup's behavior is strongly influenced by this status.

It is confusing though, how in apparent seamless fashion we accept the fact that enemies, who inflict so much pain on each other, can become friends, even allies, at another point in history. The United States and Great Britain were enemies once, and today they are the closest of friends. The same with Vietnam, Germany, Japan, Spain, Mexico, and many other nations. Does this also alert us to the possibility that our friends can become enemies? The Berlin airlift, following the Second World War, is an example of how quickly perceptions can change about ingroup and outgroup status. Just a short time before the airlift, the large group status of Germans and Russians was very different for Americans. Ultimately, the alliances of politics are organized around favoring the ingroup as conditions of common interest change. Similar fluctuations can occur between all kinds of ingroups and outgroups. For example, during the civil rights period in the United States, Jews and African Americans were aligned politically, though today relations appear less positive. These shifts can develop between religious groups, ethnic groups, gangs, mafia families, and so on, as conditions or issues of mutual interest emerge or fade. In essence, no large group alliance is permanently secure, nor should we expect that they be permanently insecure. For this reason Fromm (1941/1963) was disdainful about how easily the individual can give up his or her life for these large group identities and the causes that they promote at any given time. These shifts are also associated with Dalal's (2002) criticism of racial categories that highlight difference where difference does not truly exist. But what has transformed when these changes occur? It is not likely that anything substantial has changed about the large groups themselves.

THE NATURE OF AGGRESSION

The fluid quality of intergroup alliances has direct impact on the individual, as societal conditions demand more or less emphasis on large group identity.

The salience of collective identity demands more or less dependence upon the large group for security and self-worth, and these experiences of self in relation to the large group are what change. Our theory of human nature will influence our interpretation of these conditions, especially as it relates to prejudice. An important shift in psychoanalytic thinking has been the conceptual departure from drive and ego theory toward a lucid elaboration of object relations and the self. This shift involves important implications, not only for psychoanalysts and psychotherapists, but also potentially for culture and society. This has the potential to shape society's attitudes toward parenting, education, and views of human nature. If we consider that prejudice involves elements of aggression between individuals and identity groups, then the position we take about the role of aggression in human beings will determine our theory of prejudice.

Freud's belief about the aggressive nature of people led him to justify the negative relations he saw between groups of people. In *Civilization and its Discontents* (1930/1962), Freud expresses that, "It is clearly not easy for men to give up the satisfaction of the inclination to aggression. They do not feel comfortable without it . . ." (p. 61). From this premise he explains that,

> it is always possible to bind together a considerable number of people in love, so long as there are other people left over to receive the manifestations of their aggressiveness. (p. 61)

These statements are direct extensions of Freud's view that one aspect of our nature is aggressive and therefore intergroup hostility is to be expected. In other words, aggression and prejudice are natural aspects of who we are, and therefore they are inevitable. In the statement above we can see the compatibility of Freud's view about a basic need to have an outlet for aggression and Sumner's (1906) idea that cohesion of ingroups is associated with hostility toward outgroups. This has not been a sufficient explanation for prejudice, as research in social psychology discovered, showing that hostility toward an outgroup is not necessarily bound to cohesion of the ingroup (Duckitt, 1992; Hogg & Abrams, 1988). Although Freud recognizes the functional utility of the interrelationship between the self and the ingroup, the expectation of aggression supersedes any implications that ingroup favoritism (a relational implication) would have allowed him to pursue. Freud (1930/1962) writes,

> it would be hard for me to love him [the stranger]. Indeed, I should be wrong to do so, for my love is valued by all my own people as a sign of my preferring them, and it is an injustice to them if I put a stranger on a par with them. . . . On closer inspection, I find still further difficulties. Not merely is this stranger in general unworthy of my love; I must honestly confess that he has more claim to

my hostility and even my hatred. He seems not to have the least trace of love for me and shows me not the slightest consideration. If it will do him any good he has no hesitation in injuring me. . . . (pp. 56–57)

The literature that associates prejudice with fear is a direct outcome of the position Freud was expressing. If our expectation is that people will be aggressive, Freud's mistrust of the outgroup is logical. In his life experience Freud was witness to excessive destruction between ingroups and outgroups, and his own ingroups of Jews and Psychoanalysis were targets of prejudice. The question of whether perceptions influenced his expectations or vice versa ultimately becomes of secondary importance once he decided that aggression is a primary motivator of behavior. This view of human nature influences how we will attempt to address prejudice. Freud continues,

> The element of truth behind all this, which people are so ready to disavow, is that men are not gentle creatures who want to be loved, and who at the most can defend themselves if they are attacked; they are, on the contrary, creatures among whose instinctual endowments is to be reckoned a powerful share of aggressiveness. As a result, their neighbor is for them not only a potential helper or sexual object, but also someone who tempts them to satisfy their aggressiveness on him, to exploit his capacity for work without compensation, to use him sexually without his consent, to seize his possessions, to humiliate him, to cause him pain, to torture and to kill him. . . . The existence of this inclination to aggression, which we can detect in ourselves and justly assume to be present in others, is the factor which disturbs our relations with our neighbor. . . . (p. 58–59)

If we accept the premise that aggression is a fundamental element of human nature that must have outlets for expression, then we evaluate the outsider as a necessary object that is available to receive such aggression. The outgroup becomes a structure that has been erected in society, and in the minds of individuals, in order to facilitate our need to express aggression. We would expect nothing less in return. It is clear that this view of human nature has implications for expectations about people, which influences fundamental perceptions that do not get questioned because they meet the expectations. From this position, prejudice is an outcome of aggression and is inevitable.

If that is what we conclude, then the most we can hope for is that our nature will be suppressed by social conditions that provide less destructive outlets or authorities that completely forbid certain behaviors. Examples of ethnic aggression that was unleashed in societies that had previously appeared to establish coexisting subgroups may lead us to accept this explanation. Alternatively, Volkan (2007) suggests that in such cases we are likely to encounter enduring historical traumas shared by the various subgroups and that have become interconnected with the political, economic, and legal conditions of that society. The aggression, he believes, is a repetition of those past injustices that have eroded the capacity for basic trust between groups. This view is in line with a relational position on aggression that views it as a secondary response to frustrations and disappointments, leading to the position that prejudice is a compensation for vulnerability.

The initial relational responses to the aggressive instinct model regard aggression as a secondary response to threats upon the integrity of the self. Guntrip (1971) states, "there is reason to believe that [Freud's] theories of instinctive sex and instinctive aggression have done as much harm to our general cultural orientation in this century . . . as his opening up of the field of psychotherapy in depth has done good" (p. 137). Following this line of thought further, he continues, "It is important to get our theory of aggression right, because so many avant-garde writers are quick to make use of the idea that aggression is an innate biological instinct that ought to be expressed, and that one must be aggressive to be free and mature" (p. 139). For Guntrip, aggression is clearly a secondary reaction that is an attempt to compensate for vulnerability. From this perspective, Guntrip suggests that hate can emerge when the vulnerability is too great to allow coping. Our effort to get it right matters precisely because such theories address perceptions of experience and influence understanding of human potential in the psychotherapy room, as well as in the broader society.

Ian Suttie (1935/1988) was one of the first to reject the position that aggression is enacted for its own sake. He boldly proclaimed, "Earth hath no hate but love to hatred turned" (p. 23). If we consider aggression to be a reactive process, then our attention is directed toward the internal and external conditions that lead to frustrations and threats (Allport, 1954). Mitchell (1993) discusses the implications of advocating for one view or the other as significantly influencing clinicians. For example, he states that believing in an aggressive drive would lead to a formulation that the target of aggression, being the therapist or other individuals in the patient's life, is unjustifiably being attacked, because the aggression is an internal urge that is being projected or displaced onto the target. Recognizing that the aggression is within oneself, rather than caused by the target, would be considered therapeutic. In contrast, if aggression were viewed as reactive, then aggression itself would not be the therapeutic focus. Instead, an effort to understand the more basic threat that is frustrating and disappointing the patient receives attention. From this position the aggression is justified in terms of a pre-existing or current traumatizing event. Mitchell (1993) prefers an integrative approach to understanding aggression by acknowledging a "prewired potential that is evoked by circumstances perceived as subjectively threatening or endangering"

(p. 161). This position attends to both the universal and inevitable aspects of aggression in that an aggressive response is possible to real danger in the environment or the psyche, but it also recognizes that aggression is not a given. This offers us a chance to attend to the conditions that could initiate prejudice and actually do something about them.

In line with Mitchell's view that there is an aggressive potential that can be triggered by perceptions of internal or external conditions of threat, so too there is the potential for prejudice that can be initiated as a response to internal or external conditions. Similar to aggression, the universal potential of prejudice is an outcome of internal or external threats that promote the interchangeability of the individual and the large group. When prejudice manifests there is no differentiation between the large group and the individual, and therefore the security of both is evaluated simultaneously. It is possible to suggest that prejudice only occurs subsequent to this overidentification, following which massive splitting, rationalization, and denial occur to permit aggression without guilt.

SYNOPSIS OF DEVELOPMENTAL IMPLICATIONS

The relational paradigm encourages an elaboration of the interrelationship between autonomy and dependence needs (Josselson, 1994). This pertains to the quality of interpersonal relationships, and, importantly, we should include the manner in which people affiliate with large groups as they progress through life. As we function in society, similar needs to maintain autonomy as an individual while recognizing dependence needs with large groups and developing collective identity is paramount. This process unfolds between the individual and large groups, as it had years earlier between the infant and the caregiver. Part of the current paradigm in psychoanalysis recognizes the motivational nature of people as oriented toward social affiliation (Sullivan, 1953; Fairbairn, 1952; Mitchell, 1988). From this relational perspective in psychoanalysis, we can find similar conceptual schemes in social psychology (Allport, 1954; Brewer, 1991; Smith & Henry, 1996) and developmental psychology (Bowlby, 1969; Stern, 1985) that help to facilitate a reformulation of our understanding of prejudice.

In early adulthood the large group begins to represent an important resource for identity, security, and self-enhancement. Most individuals establish emotional relationships with large groups that are proximal and historical for their family. The manner in which this occurs varies from culture to culture, but it appears that all human beings experience their large group affiliation as a vital aspect of who they are, and this affiliation may influence behavior toward others, or the way one may be treated by others. At times the integrity of the large group is secure enough, allowing the individual to function as an autonomous being. When the intergroup condition or one's characterological disposition is insecure, then the vulnerable individual is likely to become oriented to the conditions that threaten the group and thereby the self. The continuum of reactions seems to be interrelated with the experience of threat. The apparently universal experience of ingroup favoritism may be noticed at mild to moderate levels of threat (Duckitt, 1992). Outright prejudice and hatred, an extreme reaction, is indicative of a significant psychological or physical threat.

WHAT WE LEARN FROM ATTACHMENT THEORY

The large group provides a structure from which satisfying relations with individuals are sought beyond the family. Attachment theory uses an evolutionary perspective to inform our understanding of the patterns of relating that develop between people. At the core is the functional emphasis on survival and the use of certain people to make that more likely. To that end, infants form affectional bonds with important individuals, and the quality of those bonds have implications for characterological development and subsequent capacity to form affectional bonds with other adults. Although it is clear that large groups serve a protective function for most species, the role of the large group for people was not immediately endorsed as a structure that the attachment behavioral system utilizes (Ainsworth, 1989). Attachment theory would accept that a dyadic affectional bond promotes safety and self-esteem, and can provide a needed secure base that facilitates behavior that is supported by the culture. It is not clear why identification with a large group, which can provide the same benefits of safety, self-esteem, and a secure base, should not be endorsed as a kind of affectional bond in adulthood that exists in addition to dyadic bonds.

Leaving aside the question of whether identification with a group serves the same function as the attachment to another person, we can still assess the underlying dynamics of the identification or attachment. This returns us to the examination of separation and attachment processes, also discussed as needs for closeness and distance with certain individuals. Attachment theory provides empirical support for these processes as influencing relational styles between an infant and caregiver, and between two adults. Avoidant, ambivalent, and disorganized attachments, the so-called insecure attachments, represent extreme styles of closeness and distance in relating. Secure attachment implies that an optimal balance between separation and attachment processes has been achieved. For individuals with a secure attachment history, relationships with other individuals involve expectations that commitment does not overshadow autonomy, but rather that an interdependence of the two modes operates freely (Josselsen, 1994).

Extrapolating to the large group, individuals incorporate the large group as a part of the self-concept called collective identity. An optimal balance between affiliation with the group and autonomy as an individual continues to be necessary to facilitate security. The implication is that early-life experiences that pertain to security of the infant may influence similar needs with other adults. The large group also provides a security function for the adult, and dependence upon the large group waxes and wanes based on internal or external threats and anxiety. The greater the anxiety, the more dependence upon the group for security, and less autonomy is available as an individual. At that point, psychological defenses restrict perception and other people are perceived strictly in terms of ingroup or outgroup membership.

Attachment theory's emphasis on survivability as the selection criteria throughout evolution allows us to question whether the conditions that favored group formation for survival are the same today as they have always been. Given that our perceptual reality formulates ingroups and outgroups, we can speculate that either the formation of an ingroup was important, or that our ability to identify an outgroup was important, or that both were useful. However, our discussion of these perceptual distinctions is complicated because it involves two levels of analysis simultaneously. To clarify, consider that for the individual a basic function of our brain discriminates between objects in the environment in order to organize and understand external conditions. This is the biological process that underlies the psychological potentiality of identity formation. We can surmise that identity formation is a necessary and vital aspect of self that is important, if not necessary, for each person's psychological survival. Therefore, the individual perceives ingroups and outgroups as a means of establishing a vital aspect of identity.

On the large group level, we can speculate that survival required that the large group provide security in an environment that was threatening. This would have been a protective function to keep outgroups from intruding on territory that had been staked out to provide enough land for farming and hunting, and possibly as a mode of asserting dominance so that the ingroup could be perceived as superior and strong in a threatening environment. Today, the world has become considerably more interactive and interdependent. In fact, numerous threats are global that can make all large groups insecure. It is not so clear that survivability is ensured by the same method of distinguishing between ingroups and outgroups, as it had been for so long. As conditions have significantly changed in the way large groups can interact, we can ask how these distinctions could continue to sustain the individual (in terms of identity) while simultaneously engaging new intersubjective possibilities at the intergroup level. This is especially ripe for study as bicultural and multiple identities are becoming commonplace. Can this help us to question the inevitability of prejudice?

Attachment theory gains considerable credibility from its use of ethology and evolutionary theory. The theory suggests that the attachment behavioral system provides a survival advantage by keeping the infant in proximity with a caregiver (Ainsworth, 1989). This facilitates the experience of a secure base, and only after the secure base is established can the infant feel safe enough to explore the environment. Regardless of the cultural emphasis on more or less exploration, the original interest is in the secure base with the caregiver. The initial need for a secure base is a corollary to the ingroup being established prior to perception of the outgroup (Allport, 1954). The implications for identity formation and ingroup favoritism, along with understanding the manifestation of prejudice, requires further elaboration of the large group in the mind.

SUMMARY OF THE LARGE GROUP IN THE MIND

For Fairbairn, the family is the first social group from which psychological connections with larger groups extend over time (Fairbairn, 1952). Allport (1954) discusses a similar phenomenon of concentric loyalties that extend to larger and more inclusive groups. Just as the family becomes represented in the mind of the child, so too are the large groups in the mind of the adult. Fairbairn's developmental model of mind provides a framework that is unequivocally relational, with considerable flexibility to extend beyond the dyadic interactions to which most psychoanalytic theories stay limited. This is necessary to help explain the function of prejudice in the individual. Representations of large groups in the mind reflect a dialectical interaction between the individual and the group that can shape perception, belief, emotion, and action.

Fairbairn understood that relationships are fundamentally interdependent. This means that, intrapsychically, the relationships that have been internalized represent a tension between more or less dependence. For Fairbairn, the initial relationship begins with an infantile dependence upon the caregiver. This is associated with primary identification in which there is no psychological differentiation between the caregiver and infant. Healthy development proceeds as dependence becomes a mutual experience and some degree of separation and autonomy unfolds. Psychopathology, in Fairbairnian terms, is indicative of a persistence of an infantile dependence into adulthood. This implies that the person has an underlying vulnerability, which leaves him overly dependent upon the caregiver for apparent security, but paradoxically leaves the infant, child, or adult continuously insecure and vulnerable. Much of the relationship with the caregiver becomes unconscious in order to tolerate the unsatisfying relationship. In this regard, the individual does not develop adequate balance as an autonomous person in relationship to others (Josselson, 1988). In particular, a balance does not emerge between separation and attachment processes, inhibiting a natural experience of differentiation that does not threaten to become aloneness.

Extending this theory of mind into adulthood suggests that in some cases infantile dependence and primary identification may continue to influence relationships during early adulthood. This is the time frame when establishing identifications beyond the family, with large groups, and facilitating collective identity become the primary developmental tasks. If we accept that pathology is associated with primary identification, it is indicative of a problem in differentiation between the self and other. When we apply this model to describe the relationship between the individual and the large group, we emphasize the conditions that would promote or impede a mature dependence upon the large group. Again, the optimal balance between separation and attachment processes is relevant. At the extremes, the individual struggles to maintain self-cohesion. An overidentification with the ingroup is an effort to support the self. Psychologically, it is the equivalent of a primary identification with the caregiver/ ingroup. Why is prejudice the result of an overidentification between the self and ingroup? This question leads to the convergence of concepts from attachment theory, object relations theory, and social psychology.

WARDING OFF ANNIHILATION ANXIETY

Overidentification indicates that a compensation has occurred. To understand how prejudice can emerge from this effort to care for the self, we must consider the underlying need that makes this compensation necessary. A psychological understanding about the interrelationship of the individual and large group recognizes that both the developmentally deficient person and the context-influenced person could overidentify with a large group to overcome a vulnerability. Hurvich (2003) writes that annihilation anxiety concerns the preservation of the self. At either a conscious or unconscious level, danger is present, indicating a threat to the person's survival. Relevant to the hypothesis outlined in the chapter on attachment theory, Hurvich draws attention to the increased likelihood of vulnerability associated with annihilation anxiety if the person has an insecure attachment style. In his discussion he notes that the threat to the psyche can occur early but is also possible throughout the life cycle. This suggests that environmental conditions and context can increase the perception of threat. Importantly, Hurvich posits that it is very difficult to change beliefs and behaviors when people are defending against annihilation anxiety, and this occurs with both individuals who are psychotic and nonpsychotic. This seems pertinent to the prejudiced person we are discussing for which beliefs and attitudes do not shift easily. Especially relevant to understanding the relationship to prejudice, Hurvich states that the interaction of annihilation anxiety and aggression is underappreciated. He cites a comment by Prelinger to his presentation on this topic. Prelinger states, "The degree of annihilation anxiety is a safe measure of the degree of aggressiveness . . ." (p. 602, cited in Hurvich, 2003). In the previous chapter, we discussed how the continuum of prejudicial feelings and behaviors reflect the degree to which one's life is at stake, either physically or psychologically. In other words, the degree of the perceived threat will influence the overidentification and the intensity of the expression of prejudice.

THE SOCIAL OBJECT

We can proceed with the understanding that an overidentification with a large group is a compensation for either prior or current threat and vulnerability. The notion of security is common for all theories of self. Fairbairn was especially concerned with the psychological state of withdrawal from a bad external world in an effort to find security in the inner world (Guntrip, 1969). An overidentification with a large group is a similar kind of withdrawal from bad internal or external threats. The individual withdraws into the ingroup. This clearly stops participation in a diverse world. By providing a place in the mind for the large group, we offer a way to understand how object relations that stem from dyadic contact do not cease to influence relationships with societal structures that become relevant in early adulthood and vice versa.

Hopper (2003) writes about the social unconscious as a place in the mind for the forces of culture and large groups to influence the person. He believes that if clinicians do not recognize the potential effects of these phenomena, then they will not notice when they are recreated in the clinical situation. For Hopper, the social unconscious is a bridge between sociology, group analysis, and contemporary psychoanalysis. The concept of a social object, discussed in chapter 4, identifies the large group in the mind and is congruent with Hopper's writing on the social unconscious. The social object is the large group equivalent of the object representation that is associated with important individuals and dyadic relationships. Social object representations are interdependent with pre-existing object representations; however, they can have an independent influence on perception and behavior.

The social object is interactive with collective identity, though collective identity is the conscious part of the social object. Elements that remain unconscious involve internalized social and cultural meanings that cannot be known but that influence the way one is (Hopper, 1996). An overidentification with a large group suggests that the social object is salient and influencing perception. Both developmental and contextual factors can facilitate an overidentification. The former condition is chronic, while the latter condition can affect just about anyone given the right circumstances, and is usually a transitory state. Unfortunately, some outgroups are chronically under threat, which raises questions about how to resolve intergroup conflict and personal prejudices in societies that are stratified with competing power relations. In either case, the overidentification is a compensation that utilizes the large group in an effort to shore up the experienced insecurity of the self.

The greater the threat, the more perception will be influenced by unconscious process via the social object. The implication of an overidentification is that the optimal balance between autonomy as an individual and attachment as a group member has dissolved. Instead, the individual is overly dependent upon the ingroup as a representation of self. At those times, there is more risk that ingroup favoritism can transform into hatred. This is indicative of pathology that arises when the threat to the self is severe. The fear that is felt in reaction to the danger is fundamental in initiating aggression and hatred when the anxiety is unrelenting (Suttie, 1935/1988; Guntrip, 1971). As discussed above, this is associated with either conscious or unconscious annihilation anxiety. Transient environmental conditions can feel just as threatening when periods of actual conflict erupt between large groups. Similarly, experiences of humiliation turn one's anger toward the object that is regarded to be responsible for the humiliation. All along the continuum of prejudice, from ingroup favoritism to hatred, the emphasis is on both the relationship of the individual to the ingroup and the experience of security or insecurity that overidentification brings to our attention.

WHAT IS THE NATURE OF PREJUDICE?

The implication of the question that asks about the "nature" of prejudice implies something about survivability. The answer must indicate something about how prejudice is part of a self-protective process. When prejudice is enacted the large group represents the self. At that point the individual and the group need each other to exist and survive. This is a crucial condition that initiates prejudice and dissolves the distinction between the intrapsychic and the sociological. The link between the individual and the large group is experienced psychologically in terms of collective identity, as the individual organizes and emotionally relates to various identities. This organizes multiple large groups into one dimension of the self-concept, which is oriented toward intergroup perceptions rather than interpersonal perceptions.

An optimal balance between autonomy as an individual and affiliation as a group member provides the greatest chances for tolerance of intergroup differences. When this is achieved in development, Brewer's optimal distinctiveness theory suggests that there is an ongoing tension between a need for assimilation with the group and differentiation from the group so that equilibrium is maintained. When characterological or environmental insecurity is present, the individual feels vulnerable, and there is a pull toward compensation in an effort to strengthen the self. The large group can function as a compensation structure for the individual; however, as long as the condition of vulnerability persists, the compensation must be maintained.

CASE STUDIES ON PREJUDICE

Case presentations of clinical work constantly refer to large group affiliations. It is common in most clinical presentations to introduce the patient with his or her age, marital status, race or ethnicity, and gender, then possibly the religion and country of origin, if not the United States. So we immediately categorize patients by their collective identities. This is not often pursued as a possible dynamically influential component of how the person interacts with other people of their ingroups or outgroups, or how those large group affiliations are part of the self-system.

In an early paper on prejudice, Bird (1957) introduces a White, Jewish woman who developed a short-lived, two-week prejudice toward Black men that erupted during the course of treatment. His classical understanding of prejudice is that it keeps envy and aggression from being acted out toward loved objects by venting hostility toward a displaced individual or group. From this perspective, groups are really individuals that reflect an Oedipal situation. In this case, the patient's prejudice was understood to be a projection of envy that was actually associated with her mother and sister. Bird believes that the prejudice directed at outgroups is an effort to protect a positive transference with the analyst. In other words, the prejudice toward Black men disguised her sexual impulses toward the analyst, and Bird (1957) writes, racial hatred, as a defense, operated in this way: the patient identified herself with her imagined concept of me and at the same time projected her dangerous impulses onto the persons of Negro men. As a result of this double displacement, a Negro man making advances to her represented her impulse to make advances to me. And her resentment of the supposed advances by the Negro represented the imagined resentment I would display if she gave in to her own impulses. (p. 497)

Bird suggests that prejudice in this case represented a barrier between the races, which symbolizes the gulf between the two of them. This was present in various areas, such as her being Jewish and him non-Jewish, him being an analyst and her a patient, gender difference, and so on. What is not acknowledged is that each of these "gulfs" are actual collective identities that represent the patient and analyst. We could acknowledge that she is utilizing the large group to protect herself from some vulnerability. The large group differences between the patient and analyst seem to bring this vulnerability to light. Bird's approach is to presume that prejudice is a displaced reaction to protect the self from recognizing the aggression toward a loved historical figure, or unacceptable impulses toward him. A different approach would be to acknowledge the large group implications of the reported prejudice in relation to actual differences between them that are somehow threatening. If we consider that prejudice is an outcome of an overidentification that is triggered by anxiety, we could ask ourselves whether an underlying vulnerability is historically and/or contextually driven.

The potential to overidentify as a compensation, for this patient, is hinted at by Bird when he reports that in the first session the patient had a fantasy of marrying him, suggesting a propensity to eliminate the boundary between self and other. We are alerted to the underlying potential of using the other, and we could predict the large group for self-enhancement. We can think about how the patient has eliminated the boundary between herself and the large group, and how that is both useful and debilitating in her life.

Stryker (2007) comments that meaning associated with experiences is shaped by the individual's place in social structures of class, ethnicity, gender, age, religion, and other large group categories. We should ask ourselves how collective identity, in interaction with the therapist's collective identity, can be shaping the interaction and whether the large group content is independent from the familiar interpersonal realm. Layton (2006) describes a case in which idealizing and denigrating perceptions about race permeate the clinical encounter, but importantly the perceptions also oscillate so that sometimes the patient is in the superior position in relation to his therapist and other people, and at other times he experiences himself as inferior. Layton understands this dichotomous splitting in relation to structural power relations that operate between ingroups and outgroups. She describes the prejudice that was enacted in her patient's life as a space created to overcome vulnerability. Sometimes he experienced his group as superior, but at other times he was unable to keep out the stigmatizing stereotypes about his ingroup, which left him in a position of needing to reject that aspect of himself. These experiences suggest ongoing perceptions of self and other as group members rather than two individuals. It is during moments when large group identifications are salient that prejudice can be directed at others and simultaneously experienced as an attack. Again, at those moments I would be alerted to the anxiety that may be present, either caused in the immediate interaction, precipitated by an event in his life, or as unconscious material that is newly available.

Incorporating Brewer's optimal distinctiveness model, we can understand the moments when this patient rejects his ingroup as being related to anxiety arising from feeling too assimilated with this ingroup, which triggers needs for differentiation. The negative stereotype that he associates with his ingroup would have made him sensitive to the degree that he experiences the saliency of this ingroup. At those moments there is less differentiation between himself and the group. The degree of anxiety would indicate more or less consciousness about this overidentification. When this person experiences superiority of his ingroup, we are alerted to the splitting, rationalization, and denial defenses being used to compensate for the vulnerability associated with a denigrated ingroup, but at the same time we know that the self and large group are the same for this person. One goal would be to achieve equilibrium with his ingroup identity and autonomy as an individual.

SUMMARY OF RELATIONALITY AND PREJUDICE

The relational perspective provides the framework from which to understand how and why the large group is the compensatory structure used to overcome vulnerability, and how prejudice can be a consequence. Affiliation with the large group parallels the movement toward security that was sought in early life by establishing a secure base in the attachment relationship with the caregiver. A relational explanation orients our attention to the need for the affiliation with the large group. Ideally a balance is established between the autonomous person and his or her affiliation as a group member. Prejudice is an outcome of an aberration in the affiliation with the ingroup. When an overidentification is operating there is no differentiation between the individual and large group. This is similar to Fairbairn's description of primary identification with a caregiver. The social object is the intrapsychic representation of the large group identification. Based on the degree of threat or vulnerability, it influences perception and behavior and is the unconscious aspect of collective identity. Research in social psychology has demonstrated that when collective identity is salient, depersonalization occurs, and the self becomes interchangeable with the ingroup. At that point the self and group are interdependent, and threats are perceived at both levels simultaneously. Once the ingroup is psychologically established we become aware of other large groups to which we do not belong, making the outgroup an unavoidable aspect of the environment. Unfortunately, the prejudice that can follow an overidentification with an ingroup can initiate insecurity for other groups leading to further prejudice, and a vicious cycle of vulnerability can ensue.

Given the underlying threat that an overidentification implies, perception of outgroups is filtered through a lens of vulnerability. Vulnerability is associated with defensive processes, and therefore splitting, rationalization, and denial operate to distort perceptions of others. One way to understand this is that the greater the degree of vulnerability, the more reliance on unconscious process and the social object. This simplifies the environment and promotes a homogenization of both ingroups and outgroups. It helps explain the prejudiced person's tendency to idealize or devalue the ingroup and outgroup. Perception is geared toward enhancing the self by viewing the ingroup/self as superior and good, while the outgroup is denigrated as inferior and bad.

Prejudice is the negative differentiation between people, usually based on large group identities. Although it is a destructive force in human interaction, for the individual it serves the psychological function of reducing vulnerability and enhancing self-esteem through affiliation with a community that is deemed meaningful. All individuals form attachments with a variety of large groups in the environment, which becomes important as an aspect of collective identity. The extent to which balancing the degree to which one maintains an experience of being an autonomous person while simultaneously experiencing belonging to a large group can promote tolerance of differences.

FUTURE DIRECTIONS

Focusing on identity as the variable that helps us address prejudice brings together diverse literatures. An important piece of the puzzle is offered by structural symbolic interactionism, which focuses on the linking of social interaction to roles and identities. Stryker (2007) explains that the diversity of parts of society are organized in multiple and overlapping ways that are interactional, functional, and hierarchical. These parts of society can be relatively independent, or at times interdependent, and at other times conflicting, and still other times cooperative. A central premise of this perspective is that self reflects society. This permits a parallel conceptualization that recognizes diverse parts of the self as independent of each other, at other times interdependent, at still other times conflicting, all the while potentially being mutually reinforcing (Stryker, 2007). Behavior is an outcome of role choices that structural symbolic interactionism attributes to identity salience, which makes that identity psychologically central. Although this perspective places emphasis on the external conditions that highlight a particular identity, I would include internal states that are developmentally influenced. This theory is built on James' (1890) theory of multiple selves, which importantly, from the symbolic interactionist perspective, reflect multiple identities. The relevance of this perspective to the psychoanalytic literature on multiple selves is striking. Bromberg (1998) writes about the capacity to feel like one self while being many. Similarly, Sullivan (1964) comments, "For all I know every human being has as many personalities as he has interpersonal relations" (p. 221). The difference between symbolic interactionism and interpersonal psychoanalysis is that the former emphasizes the involvement of the person within a hierarchy of large groups that are organized in some fashion. Interpersonal psychoanalysis regards the central focus to be the interpersonal sphere and, as Bromberg (1998) puts it, "the ability to stand in the spaces between realities without losing any of them" (p. 186).

Allport believes that there is no intrinsic reason that loyalties to grand identities cannot be equally important to an individual, as are the close and personal affiliations of intimate dyadic relationships. Allport's idea synthesizes the sociological and psychoanalytic perspectives offered by Stryker and Sullivan, with significant implications for the study of prejudice. I am referring to the importance of attending to the personally relevant identities that each individual incorporates locally, while finding a way for a superordinate identity to remain satisfying, not assimilating so much, so as to initiate what Brewer refers to as the need for differentiation. For example, race is a dominant loyalty for many people, and it is a source of tension as various "races" struggle for dominance. Allport asks in 1954, "Can a loyalty to mankind be fashioned before interracial warfare breaks out?" (p. 43). Somehow he is hopeful that we can learn to utilize the potential of attachments to more inclusive identities, such as humankind, while maintaining loyalties to identity groups that are historically and personally relevant. This broader superordinate identity is often cited as an antidote to prejudice. We still have a long way to proceed; however, evolution of people and societies inches toward this goal.

Elaborating upon the implications of Allport's comments on multiple group loyalties has recently become a central focus in social cognitive psychology. Self-categorization theory predicts that beliefs about a particular large group identity will influence how a person will behave when that identity is salient

(Turner, Hogg, Oakes, Reicher, & Wetherell, 1987; Reynolds, Turner, Haslam, & Ryan, 2001). For instance, if I believe that my ingroup is tolerant, when this collective identity is salient I am likely to think or act tolerantly (Verkuyten & Hagendoorn, 1998). Along similar lines of thinking, Reynolds and colleagues (2001) state that the salience of particular collective identities could change the likelihood of prejudice. These researchers suggest that such findings de-emphasize personality variables in predicting prejudice. This is a hopeful indi-cation that it may be possible to shape prejudicial attitudes in positive directions by highlighting specific aspects of collective identities.

MULTIPLE SELVES AND MULTIPLE IDENTITIES

Throughout this book, discussion was simplified in terms of one ingroup in re-lation to one outgroup. In certain contexts this is exactly how people evaluate themselves and others, especially when threat and anxiety are present; how-ever, we all know that people are also much more complicated. Recently, mod-els have been introduced that acknowledge the complexity of the self. These efforts recognize the multiple large group affiliations that all individuals inte-grate into a self-system, and the varied experience of self that is part of that process. One trajectory that emerged recognizes the need for personal sub-group affiliations, while exploring the possibility of accepting a super-ordinate identity that may reduce prejudice (Gaertner, Dovidio, Anastasio, Bachman, & Rust, 1993). These models conclude that we cannot simply im-pose a superordinate identity on ingroups and outgroups and expect prejudice to recede. Instead, evidence is accumulating that it is important to respect sub-group identities while developing an acceptable superordinate identity that is also valued (Gaertner & Dovidio, 2000; Hornsey & Hogg, 2000; Amiot, de la Sablonniere, Terry, & Smith, 2007; Volkan, 2002). In fact, Hornsey and Hogg (2000) and Volkan (2002) warn that when there is a threat to subgroup iden-tity, the individual's need for distinctiveness can become aggressive.

Roccas and Brewer (2002) move much closer to the potential integration of an intrapsychic model with a social cognitive model. They elaborate the implications of varying degrees of overlap that occur between different sub-groups in a self-system. This is especially congruent with notions of self-states in psychoanalysis and may offer new ways to discuss the simultaneous experience of continuity of the self in relation to transient self-states. Roccas and Brewer (2002) discuss a cognitive model on a continuum that increases in complexity from a single representation of self (one ingroup) to a level of complexity that is inclusive of multiple subgroups while also sustaining the relevance of the lower-level identity. They write that social identity complexity is cognitively complex in that the individual is aware of the overlap between some of his or her subgroup identities and other subgroup identities. This kind of cross-categorization can lead to awareness that many individuals may be both ingroup members on some dimensions and simultaneously outgroup members on other dimensions. Roccas and Brewer write that this kind of social identity complexity can lead to a reduction of prejudice. This literature offers a bridge to discuss the relationship between multiple self-states and multiple social identities, and can lead to a better understanding of multiple group loyalties.

CONCLUSION

A new psychoanalytic perspective on prejudice requires a return to the original interdisciplinary collaboration of the 1950s. Rather than focusing on either individual differences or on intergroup processes, the effort to elaborate the simultaneous influences and consequences of both realms of experience would stimulate a resurgence of efforts that re-engage both psychoanalytic and social psychological perspectives. The anxieties of living impose considerable demands on individuals and the groups to which they are bound. In clinical work, the effort to change is a hopeful event, and trajectories of life paths shift in positive ways often enough to keep both therapists and patients hopeful. The same can be true for societies as trajectories and improvements develop, expectedly in slow fashion, to offer more people a secure place from which to participate in their lives. The evolution of societal structures has changed in the last century in ways that permit ongoing and interdependent interaction between large groups. This has resulted in both positive and negative possibilities that may offer a fresh way to attend to the problem of prejudice. The pseudospeciation that Erikson discussed as the impediment to reduction of prejudice is clearer than ever as we see the variety of cultural styles present, but it is also less rigid as we cannot help but be aware of the similarities and common interests. Paradoxically, these threats may make it possible to recognize the cooperative potential that is shared by all the individuals who make up the various large groups. Within individuals or between whole societies, the boundary between the individual and large group depends upon security. Prejudice could be shifted as parenting, education, and support for the optimal balance between the individual and large group is valued and efforts are made to facilitate this experience.

.

References

Aboud, F. E. (2003). The formation of ingroup favoritism and outgroup prejudice in young children: Are they distinct attitudes? *Developmental Psychology, 39*, 48–60.

Adorno, T. W., Frenkel-Brunswik, E., Levinson, D. J., & Sanford, R. N. (1950). *The authoritarian personality*. New York: Harper & Row.

Ainsworth, M. D. S. (1982). Retrospect and prospect. In C. M. Parkes & J. Stevenson-Hinde (Eds.). *The place of attachment in human behavior* (pp. 3–30). New York: Basic Books.

Ainsworth, M. D. (1989). Attachments beyond infancy. *American Psychologist, 44*, 709–716.

Ainsworth, M. D. S., Blehar, M. C., Waters, E., & Wall, S. (1978). *Patterns of attachment: A psychological study of the strange situation*. Hillsdale, NJ: Erlbaum.

Akhtar, S. (1999). *Immigration and identity: Turmoil, treatment, and transformation*. Northvale, NJ: Jason Aronson.

Akhtar, S. (2006). Technical challenges faced by the immigrant analyst. *Psychoanalytic Quarterly, 75*, 21–43.

Akhtar, S. (2007). From unmentalized xenophobia to messianic sadism: Some reflections on the phenomenology of prejudice. In H. Parens, A. Mahfouz, S. Twemlow, & D. Scharff (Eds.). *The future of prejudice: Psychoanalysis and the prevention of prejudice* (pp. 7–19). Lanham, MD: Rowman & Littlefield.

Allport, G. (1954). *The nature of prejudice*. New York: Doubleday.

Altemeyer, B. (1981). *Right-wing authoritarianism*. Winnipeg: University of Manitoba Press.

Altemeyer, B. (1988). *Enemies of Freedom: Understanding right-wing authoritarianism*. San Francisco, CA: Jossey-Bass.

Altman, N. (1995). *The analyst in the inner city: Race, class, and culture through a psychoanalytic lens*. New Jersey: Analytic Press.

Altman, N. (2006). Whiteness. *Psychoanalytic Quarterly, 75*, 45–72.

Amiot, C. E., de la Sablonniere, R., Terry, D. J., & Smith, J. R. (2007). Integration of social identities in the self: Toward a cognitive-developmental model. *Personality and Social Psychology Review, 11*, 364–388.

Arendt, H. (1963). *Eichmann in Jerusalem: A report on the banality of evil*. New York: Viking Press.

Aronson, S. (2007). Balancing the fiddler on my roof: On wearing a yarmulke and working as a psychoanalyst. *Contemporary Psychoanalysis, 43*, 451–459.

Aviram, R. B. (2002). An object relations theory of prejudice: Defining pathological prejudice. *Journal for the Psychoanalysis of Culture and Society, 7*, 305–312.

Aviram, R. B. (2005). The social object and the pathology of prejudice. In J. S. Scharff & D. E. Scharff (Eds.). *The Legacy of Fairbairn and Sutherland* (pp. 227–236). New York: Routledge.

Aviram, R. B. (2007). Object relations and prejudice: From in-group favoritism to outgroup hatred. *International Journal of Applied Psychoanalytic Studies, 4*, 4–14.

Aviram, R. B., Brodsky, B., & Stanley, B. (2006). Borderline personality disorder, stigma, and treatment implications. *Harvard Review of Psychiatry, 14*, 249–256.

Aviram, R. B., & Rosenfeld, S. (2002). Application of social identity theory in group therapy with stigmatized adults. *International Journal of Group Psychotherapy, 52*, 121–130.

Baldwin, M. W., Keelan, J. P. R., Fehr, B., Enns, V., & Koh-Rangarajoo, E. (1996). Social cognitive conceptualization of attachment styles: Availability and accessibility effects. *Journal of Personality and Social Psychology, 61*, 94–109.

Bar-Tal, D. (1996). Development of social categories and stereotypes in early childhood: The case of "the Arab" concept formation, stereotype and attitudes by Jewish children in Israel. *International Journal of Intercultural Relations, 20*, 341–370.

Bartholomew, K., & Horowitz, L. M. (1991). Attachment styles among young adults: A test of a four-category model. *Journal of Personality and Social Psychology, 61*, 226–244.

Benjamin, J. (1995). *Like subjects, love objects*. New Haven: Yale University Press.

Bettelheim, B., & Janowitz, M. (1950). *Social change and prejudice*. New York: Free Press of Glencoe.

Bion, W. R. (1959). *Experiences in groups*. London: Tavistock Publications.

Bird, B. (1957). A consideration of the etiology of prejudice. *Journal of the American Psychoanalytic Association, 5*, 490–513.

Blass, R. B., & Blatt, S. J. (1992). Attachment and separateness: A theoretical context for the integration of object relations theory with self psychology. *Psychoanalytic Study of the Child, 47*, 189–203.

Blatt, S. J. (1990). Interpersonal relatedness and self-definition: Two personality configurations and their implication for psychopathology and psychotherapy. In J. L. Singer (Ed.). *Repression and dissociation: Implications for personality theory, psychopathology and health* (pp. 299–335). Chicago: University of Chicago Press.

Blatt, S. J., & Shichman, S. (1983). Two primary configurations of psychopathology. *Psychoanalysis and Contemporary Thought, 6*, 187–254.

Blos, P. (1967). The second individuation process of adolescence. *The psychoanalytic study of the child, 22*, 162–186.

Bodnar, S. (2004). Remembering where you come from: Dissociative process in multicultural individuals. *Psychoanalytic Dialogues, 14*, 581–604.

Bonovitz, C. (2005). Locating culture in the psychic field: Transference and countertransference as cultural products. *Contemporary Psychoanalysis, 41*, 55–76.

Bonovitz, C. (In press). Mixed race and the negotiation of racialized selves: Developing the capacity for internal conflict. *Psychoanalytic Dialogues.*

Bowen, M. (1978). *Family therapy in clinical practice*. New York: Aronson.

Bowlby, J. (1969). *Attachment and loss*. New York: Basic Books

Bowlby, J. (1973). *Separation, anxiety and anger*. New York: Basic Books.

Bowlby, J. (1977). The making and breaking of affectional bonds: II. Some principles of psychotherapy. *British Journal of Psychiatry, 130*, 421–431.

Bowlby, J. (1988). *A secure base*. New York: Basic Books.

Brewer, M. B. (1991). The social self: On being the same and different at the same time. *Personality and Social Psychology Bulletin, 17*, 475–482.

Brewer, M. B. (1999). The psychology of prejudice: In-group love or out-group hate? *Journal of Social Issues, 55*, 429–444.

Brewer, M. B. (2007). The importance of being we: Human nature and intergroup relations. *American Psychologist, 62*, 728–738.

Brewer, M. B., & Gardner, W. (1996). Who is this "we"? Levels of collective identity and self representation. *Journal of Personality and Social Psychology, 71*, 83–93.

Bromberg, P. M. (1998). *Standing in the spaces*. Hillsdale, NJ: Analytic Press.

Brown, R., & Zagefka, H. (2005). Ingroup affiliation and prejudice. In J. Dovidio, P. Glick, & L. Rudman (Eds.). *The nature of prejudice: Fifty years after Allport*, (pp. 54–70). Malden, MA: Blackwell.

Buechler, S. (2004), *Clinical values: Emotions that guide psychoanalytic treatment*. Hillsdale, NJ: Analytic Press.

Byng-Hall, J. (1999). *Handbook of attachment: Theory, research, and clinical*. (Ed. J. Cassidy and P. Shaver) New York, NY: Guilford Press.

Campos, J., Barrett, K., Lamb, M., Goldsmith, H., & Stenberg, C. (1983). Socioemotional development. In M. Haith & J. Campos (Eds.). *Infancy and developmental psychobiology. Vol. II. Handbook of child psychology* (pp. 783–915). New York: Wiley.

Chodorow, N. (1978). *The reproduction of mothering*. Berkeley: University of California Press.

Collins, N. L., & Read, S. J. (1990). Adult attachment, working models and relationship quality in dating couples. *Journal of Personality and Social Psychology, 58*, 644–663.

Collins, N. L., & Read, S. J. (1994). Cognitive representations of attachment: The structure and function of working models. In K. Bartholomew and D. Perlman, (Eds.). *Attachment processes in adulthood* (pp. 53–92). London: Jessica Kingsley.

Comas-Diaz, L., & Jacobsen, F. M. (1987). Ethnocultural identification in psychotherapy. *Psychiatry, 50*, 232–241.

Cooper, C. R., Grotevant, H. D. & Condon, S. M. (1983). Individuality and connectedness in the family as a context for adolescent identity formation and role-taking skill. In R. H. Grotevant & C. R. Cooper (Eds.). *New Directions for Child Development, Vol. 22. Adolescent development in the family* (pp. 43–59). San Francisco, CA: Jossey-Bass.

Cushman, P. (1995). *Constructing the self, constructing America: A cultural history of psychotherapy*. Reading, MA: Addison-Wesley.

Dalal, F. (2002). *Race, colour and the processes of racialization: New perspectives from group analysis, psychoanalysis and sociology*. Hove, England: Brunner-Routledge.

Dalal, F. (2006). Racism: Processes of detachment, dehumanization, and hatred. *Psychoanalytic Quarterly, 75*, 131–161.

Diagnostic and Statistical Manual of Mental Disorders-IV. (1994). Washington, D.C.: American Psychiatric Association.

Dollard, J., Doob, L. W., Miller, N. E., Mowrer, O. H., & Sears, R. R. (1939). *Frustration and Aggression*. New Haven: Yale University Press.

Dovidio, J. F., Glick, P., & Budman, L. A. (2005). *On the nature of prejudice: Fifty years after Allport*. Malden, MA: Blackwell.

Dovidio, J. F., Kawakami, K., & Gaertner, S. L. (2000). Reducing contemporary prejudice: Combating explicit and implicit bias at the individual and the group level. In S. Oskamp (Ed.). *The Claremont Symposium: Reducing prejudice* (pp. 137–163). Hillsdale, NJ: Erlbaum.

Duckitt, J. (1989). Authoritarianism and group identification: A new view of an old construct. *Political Psychology, 10*, 63–84.

Duckitt, J. (1992). *The social psychology of prejudice*. New York: Praeger Publishers.

Erikson, E. H. (1950). *Childhood and society*. New York: Norton.

Erikson, E. H. (1956). The problem of ego identity. *Journal of the American Psychoanalytic Association, 4*, 56–121.

Erikson, E. H. (1959/1980). *Identity and the life cycle*. New York: Norton.

Erikson, E. H. (1968). *Identity: Youth and crisis*. New York: Norton.

Erikson, E. H. (1985). Pseudospeciation in the nuclear age. *Political Psychology, 6*, 213–217.

Fairbairn, W. R. D. (1935/1952). The sociological significance of communism considered in light of psychoanalysis. *British Journal of Medical Psychology*, XV, part 3. Reprinted in *Psychoanalytic studies of the personality* (pp 233–246). New York: Routledge.

Fairbairn, W. R. D. (1946/1952). Object relationships and dynamic structure. In *Psychoanalytic studies of the personality* (pp 137–151). London: Tavistock/Routledge.

Fairbairn, W. R. D. (1952). *Psychoanalytic studies of the personality*. New York: Routledge.

Feeney, J. A., & Noller, P. (1990). Attachment style and predictor of adult romantic relationships. *Journal of Personality and Social Psychology, 58*, 281–291.

Fonagy, P. & Higgitt, A. (2007). The development of prejudice: An attachment theory hypothesis explaining its ubiquity. In H. Parens, A. Mahfouz, S. Twemlow, & D. Scharff (Eds.). *The future of prejudice: Psychoanalysis and the prevention of prejudice* (pp. 63–79). Lanham, MD: Rowman & Littlefield.

Foulkes, S. H. (1948/1983). *Introduction to group analytic psychotherapy*. William Heinemann Medical Books. London: Karnac Books.

Freud, S. (1921). *Group Psychology and the Analysis of the Ego*. New York: Norton.

Freud, S. (1926). Address to the Society of B'nai B'rith. The standard edition of the Complete Psychological works of Sigmund Freud (translated from German). *Strachney Journal*, 20, 271–274. London: The Hogarth Press and the Institute of Psychoanalysis, 1961.

Freud, S. (1930/1962). *Civilization and its discontents.* New York: Norton.

Freud, S. (1931). Libidinal types. *Standard Edition 21*, 215–220.

Freud, S. (1935/1963). *An autobiographical study.* New York: Norton.

Freud, S. (1939). *Civilization, war and death: Selection from three works by Sigmund Freud.* J. Rickman (Ed.). London: Hogarth Press and the Institute of Psychoanalysis.

Fromm, E. (1941/1963). *Escape from freedom.* New York: Holt, Rinehart, & Winston.

Fromm, E. (1947/1966). *Man for himself: An inquiry into the psychology of ethics.* New York: Fawcett.

Fromm, E. (1955/1966). *The sane society.* Greenwich, CT: Fawcett.

Fromm, E. (1973). *The anatomy of human destructiveness.* New York: Holt, Rinehart, & Winston.

Gaertner, S., & Dovidio, J. F. (1986). The aversive form of racism. In J. F. Dovidio & S. Gaertner (Eds.). *Prejudice, discrimination, and racism* (pp. 61–90). New York: Academic Press.

Gaertner, S. L., Dovidio, J. F., Anastasio, P. A., Bachman, B. A., & Rust, M. C. (1993). The common ingroup identity model: Recategorization and the reduction of intergroupbias. *European Review of Social Psychology, 4*, 1–26.

Gergen, K. J. (1971). *The concept of self.* New York: Holt, Rinehart, & Winston.

Gilligan, C. (1982). *In a different voice: Psychological theory and women's development.* Cambridge, MA: Harvard University Press.

Goffman, E. (1963). *Stigma: Notes on the management of spoiled identity.* New York: Simon & Schulster.

Greenberg, J. R., & Mitchell, S. A. (1983). *Object relations in psychoanalytic theory.* Cambridge, MA: Harvard University Press.

Grossmann, K., Grossmann, K. E., Spangler, G., Suess, G., & Unzner, L. (1985). Maternal sensitivity and newborns' orientation responses as related to quality of attachment in northern Germany. In I. Bretherton, & E. Waters (Eds.). *Growing points of attachment theory and research. Monographs of the society for research in child development, 50*, 233–298.

Grotevant, H. D., & Cooper, C. R. (1986). Individuation in family relationships: A perspective on individual differences in the development of identity and role-taking skill in adolescence. *Human Development, 29*, 82–100.

Guntrip, H. (1969). *Schizoid phenomena, object relation and the self.* New York: International Universities Press.

Guntrip, H. (1971). *Psychoanalytic theory, therapy, and the self.* New York: Basic Books.

Hamer, F. M. (2002). Guards at the gate: Race, resistance, and psychic reality. *Journal of the American Psychoanalytic Association, 50 (4)*, 1219–1238.

Hamer, F. M. (2006). Racism as a transference state: Episodes of racial hostility in the psychoanalytic context. *Psychoanalytic Quarterly, 75*, 197–214.

Hazan, C., & Shaver, P. R. (1987). Romantic love conceptualized as an attachment process. *Journal of Personality and Social Psychology, 52*, 511–524.

Hogg, M. A., & Abrams, D. (1988). *Social identifications: A psychology of intergroup relations and group processes*. London: Routledge.

Holmes, J. (1996). *Attachment, intimacy, autonomy: Using attachment theory in adult psychotherapy*. Northvale, NJ: Jason Aronson.

Hopper, E. (1996). The social unconscious in clinical work. *Group, 20, 1*, 7–42.

Hopper, E. (2003). *The social unconscious*. London: Jessica Kingsley.

Horney, K. (1939). *New ways in psychoanalysis*. New York: W. W. Norton.

Hornsey, M. J., & Hogg, M. A. (2000). Assimilation and diversity: An integrative model of subgroup relations. *Personality and Social Psychology Review, 4*, 143–156.

Hurvich, M. (2003). The place of annihilation anxiety in psychoanalytic theory. *Journal of the American Psychoanalytic Association, 51*, 579–616

James, W. (1890). *Principles of psychology*. New York: Holt.

Josselson, R. (1988). The embedded self: I and thou revisited. In D. Lapsley & F. Power (Eds.). *Self, ego, and identity* (pp. 91–106). New York: Springer-Verlag.

Josselson, R. (1994). Identity and relatedness in the life cycle. In H. Bosma, T. Graafsma, H. Grotevant, & D. De Levita (Eds.). *Identity and development: An interdisciplinary approach*. Thousand Oaks, CA: Sage Publications.

Jost, J. T., & Hamilton, D. L. (2005). Stereotypes in our culture. In J. Dovidio, P. Glick, & L. Rudman (Eds.). *The nature of prejudice: Fifty years after Allport*, (pp. 208–224). Malden, MA: Blackwell.

Kaitz, M., Bar-Haim, Y., Lehrer, M., & Grossman, E. (2004). Adult attachment style and interpersonal distance. *Attachment and Human Development, 6*, 285–304.

Katz, I. (1981). *Stigma: A social psychological analysis*. Hillsdale, NJ: Lawrence Erlbaum.

Keefe, S. E. (1992). Ethnic identity: The domain of perceptions of and attachment to ethnic groups and cultures. *Human Organization, 51*, 35–43.

Kelman, H. C. (1999). The interdependence of Israeli and Palestinian national identities: The role of the other in existential conflicts. *Journal of Social Issues, 55*, 581–600.

Kohut, H. (1971). *The analysis of the self*. New York: International Universities Press.

Kohut, H. (1985). *Self psychology and the humanities: Reflections on a new psychoanalytic approach*. New York: W. W. Norton.

Kuhn, M. H., & McPartland, T. S. (1954). An empirical investigation of self-attitude. *American Sociological Review, 19*, 68–76.

Layton, L. (2006). Racial identity, racial enactments, and normative unconscious processes. *Psychoanalytic Quarterly, 75*, 237–269.

Leary, K. (1997). Race, self-disclosure, and "forbidden talk": Race and ethnicity in contemporary clinical practice. *Psychoanalytic Quarterly, 66*, 163–189.

Leary, K. (2000). Racial enactments in dynamic treatment. *Psychoanalytic Dialogues, 10*, 639–654.

LeVine, R. A., & Campbell, D. T. (1972). *Ethnocentrism: Theories of conflict, ethnic attitudes and group behavior*. New York: Wiley.

Lewis, H.B. (1971). *Shame and guilt in neurosis*. New York: International Universities Press.

Luhtanen, R., & Crocker, J. (1992). A collective self-esteem scale: Self-evaluation of one's social identity. *Personality and Social Psychology Bulletin, 18*, 302–318.

Lyons-Ruth, K. (1991). Rapprochement or approchement: Mahler's theory reconsidered from the vantage point of recent research on early attachment relationships. *Psychoanalytic Psychology, 8*, 1–23.

Lyons-Ruth, K. (1996). Attachment relationships among children with aggressive behavior problems: The role of disorganized early attachment patterns. *Journal of Consulting and Clinical Psychology, 64*, 32–40.

Mackie, D. M., & Smith, E. R. (1998). Intergroup relations: Insights from a theoretically integrative approach. *Psychological Review, 105*, 499–529.

Mahler, M. S., Pine, F., & Bergman, A. (1975). *The psychological birth of the human infant*. New York: Basic Books.

Main, M., & Solomon, J. (1990). Procedures for identifying infants as disorganized/disoriented during the Ainsworth Strange Situation. In M. Greenberg, D. Cicchetti, & M. Cummings (Eds.). *Attachment in the preschool years: Theory, research and intervention* (pp. 121–160). Chicago: University of Chicago Press.

Marmarosh, C. L., & Corazzini, J. G. (1997). Putting the group in your pocket: Using collective identity to enhance personal and collective self-esteem. *Group Dynamics: Theory, Research, and Practice, 1*, 65–74.

May, R. (1972). *Power and innocence*. New York: Norton.

Merton, R. K. (1957). *Social theory & social structure*. New York: Free Press at Glencoe.

Mikulincer, M., & Erev, I. (1991). Attachment style and the structure of romantic love. *British Journal of Social Psychology, 30*, 273–291.

Mikulincer, M. & Shaver, P. R. (2001). Attachment theory and intergroup bias: Evidence that priming the secure base schema attenuates negative reactions to outgroups. *Journal of Personality and Social Psychology, 81*, 97–115.

Miller, D. T., & Turnbull, W. (1986). Expectancies and interpersonal processes. *Annual Review of Psychology, 37, 233*–256.

Minuchin, S. (1974). *Families and family therapy*. Cambridge, MA: Harvard University Press.

Mitchell, S. A. (1988). *Relational concepts in psychoanalysis*. Cambridge, MA: Harvard University Press.

Mitchell, S. A. (1993). *Hope and dread in psychoanalysis*. New York: Basic Books.

Moss, D. (2003). *Hating in the first person plural: Psychoanalytic essays racism, homophobia, misogyny, and terror*. New York: Other Press.

Newman, L. S., & Caldwell, T. L. (2005). Allport's "living inkblots": The role of defensive projection in stereotyping and prejudice. In J. Dovidio, P. Glick, & L. Rudman (Eds.). *The nature of prejudice: Fifty years after Allport* (pp. 377–392). Boston: Blackwell.

Ng, S. H. (1985). Biases in reward allocation resulting from personal status, group status, and allocation procedure. *Australian Journal of Psychology, 37*, 297–307.

Ng, S. H. (1986). Equity, intergroup bias and interpersonal bias in reward allocation. *European Journal of Social Psychology, 16*, 239–255.

Ng, S. H. (1989). Intergroup behaviour and the self. *New Zealand Journal of Psychology, 18*, 1– 12.

O'Leary, J. V., & Watson, R. I. (1995). Paranoia. In M. Lionells, J. Fiscalini, C. Mann, & D. Stern. *Handbook of interpersonal psychoanalysis* (pp. 397–417). Hillsdale, NJ: Analytic Press.

Palladino-Schultheiss, D., & Blustein, D. L. (1994). Contributions of family relationship factors to the identity formation process. *Journal of Counseling and Development, 73*, 159–166.

Parens, H. (2007). The roots of prejudice: Findings from observational research. In H. Parens, A. Mahfouz, S. Twemlow, & D. Scharff (Eds.). *The Future of Prejudice* (pp. 81–96). Lanham, MD: Rowman & Littlefield.

Pyszczynski, T., Solomon, S., & Greenberg, J. (2003). *In the wake of 9/11: The psychology of terror.* Washington, D.C.: American Psychological Association.

Reich, W. (1933/1972). *Character analysis*, trans. V. R. Carfagno. New York: Farrar, Straus and Giroux.

Reynolds, K. J., Turner, J. C., Haslam, S. A., & Ryan, M. K. (2001). The role of personality and group factors in explaining prejudice. *Journal of Experimental Social Psychology, 37*, 427–434.

Rice, K. G. (1990). Attachment in adolescence: A narrative and meta-analytic review. *Journal of Youth and Adolescence, 19*, 511–538.

Rice, K. G., FitzGerald, D. P., Whaley, T. J., & Gibbs, C. L. (1995). Cross-sectional and longitudinal examination of attachment, separation-individual, and college student development. *Journal of Counseling and Development, 73*, 463–474.

Robins, E. M., & Foster, D. (1994). Social identity versus personal identity: An investigation into the interaction of group and personal status with collective self-esteem on ingroup favouritism. *South African Journal of Psychology, 24*, 115–121.

Roccas, S., & Brewer, M. B. (2002). Social identity complexity. *Personality and Social Psychology Review, 2*, 88–106.

Rokeach, M. (1964). *The Three Christs of Ypsilanti.* New York: Vintage.

Rokeach, M. (1968). *Beliefs attitudes and values.* San Francisco, CA: Jossey-Bass

Rothbaum, F., Weisz, J., Pott, M., Miyake, K., & Morelli, G. (2000). Attachment and culture: Security in the United States and Japan. *American Psychologist, 55*, 1093–1104.

Rubens, R. L. (1994). Fairbairn's structural theory. In J. S. Grotstein & D. B. Rinsley (Eds.). *Fairbairn and the origins of object relations* (pp. 151–173). London: Free Association Books.

Sherif, M. Harvey, O. J., White, B. J. Hood, W., & Sherif, C. (1961/1988). *Intergroup conflict and cooperation: The robbers cave experiment.* Norman, OK: Univeristy of Oklahoma Institute of Intergroup Relations.

Smith, E. R., & Henry, S. (1996). An in-group becomes part of the self: Response time evidence. *Personality and Social Psychology Bulletin, 22*, 635–642.

Smith, E. R., Murphy, J., & Coats, S. (1999). Attachment to groups: Theory and measurement. *Journal of Personality and Social Psychology, 77*, 94–110.

Spitz, R. (1965). *The First Year of Life*. New York: International Universities Press.

Stephan, W. G., & Renfro, C. L. (2003). The role of threat in intergroup relations. In D. M. Mackie and E. R. Smith (Eds.). *From prejudice to intergroup emotions: Differentiated reactions to social groups* (pp. 191–207). New York: Psychology Press.

Stern, D. N. (1985). The interpersonal world of the infant. New York: Basic Books.

Strenger, C. (2007). Belief systems, identity, and the function of prejudice in Israeli politics. In H. Parens, A. Mahfouz, S. Twemlow, & D. Scharff (Eds.). *The future of prejudice: Psychoanalysis and the prevention of prejudice* (pp. 208–216). Lanham, MD: Rowman & Littlefield.

Stroufe, L. A., & Waters, E. (1977). Attachment as an organizational construct. *Child Development, 48*, 1184–1199.

Stryker, S. (2007). Identity theory and personality theory: Mutual relevance. *Journal of Personality, 75*, 1083–1102.

Sullaway, M., & Dunbar, E. (1996). Clinical manifestations of prejudice in psychotherapy: toward a strategy of assessment and treatment. *Clinical Psychology and Science Practice, 3*, 296–309.

Sullivan, H. S. (1953). *The interpersonal theory of psychiatry*. New York: Norton.

Sullivan, H. S. (1964). *The fusion of psychiatry and social science*. New York: Norton.

Sumner, W. G. (1906). *Folkways*. Boston: Ginn.

Suttie, I. D. (1935/1988). *The origins of love and hate*. London: Free Association.

Tajfel, H. (1969). Cognitive aspects of prejudice. *Journal of Social Issues, 25*, 79–97.

Tajfel, H., Billig, M., Bundy, R. P., & Flament, C. (1971). Social categorization and intergroup behaviour. *European Journal of Social Psychology, 1*, 149–177.

Tajfel, H., & Turner, J. C. (1986). The social identity theory of intergroup behaviour. In S. Worchel and W. G. Austin (Eds.). *Psychology of intergroup relations*. Chicago: Nelson-Hall.

Teicholz, J. G. (2006). Qualities of engagement and the analyst's theory. *International Journal of Psychoanalytic Self Psychology, 1*, 47–77.

Thompson, C. M. (1964). *Interpersonal psychoanalysis*. New York: Basic Books.

Trafimow, D., Triandis, H. C., & Goto, S. G. (1991). Some tests of the distinction between the private and collective self. *Journal of Personality and Social Psychology, 60*, 649–655.

Triandis, H. C. (1995). *Individualism and collectivism*. San Francisco, CA: Westview Press.

Triandis, H. C., Bontempo, R., Villareal, M. J., Asai, M., & Lucca, N. (1988). Individualism and collectivism: Cross-cultural perspectives on self-ingroup relationships. *Journal of Personality and Social Psychology, 54*, 323–338.

Turner, J. C. (1982). Towards a cognitive redefinition of the social group. In H. Tajfel (Ed.) *Social identity and intergroup relations* (pp. 15–40). Cambridge: Cambridge University Press.

Turner, J. C., Hogg, M. A., Oakes, P. J., Reicher, S. D., & Wetherell, M. (1987). *Rediscovering the social group: A self-categorization theory*. Oxford: Blackwell.

Vedantam, S. (2005, December 10). Psychiatry ponders whether extreme bias can be an illness. *The Washington Post*, p. A01.

Verkuyten, M., & Hagendoorn, L. (1998). Prejudice and self-categorization: The variable role of authoritarianism and in-group stereotypes. *Personality & Social Psychology Bulletin, 24*, 99–110.

Volkan, V. D. (1988). *The need to have enemies and allies: From clinical practice to international relationships.* Northvale, NJ: Jason Aronson.

Volkan, V. D. (May 10, 2002). *Large-group identity: Border psychology and related societal processes.* Paper presented at the German Psychoanalytic Association Annual Meeting, Leipzig, Germany.

Volkan, V. D. (June, 2007). Societal well-being after experiencing trauma at the hand of "Others": The interviewing of political, economic and other visible factors with hidden psychological processes affecting victimized populations. Paper presented at the Organization for Economic Cooperation and Development Conference, Measuring and Fostering the Progress of Societies, Istanbul, Turkey.

Walls, G. B. (2004). Toward a critical global psychoanalysis. *Psychoanalytic Dialogues, 14*, 605–634.

Waters, E., & Cummings, E. M. (2000). A secure base from which to explore close relationships. *Child Development, 71*, 164–172.

Weiner, M. F. (1982). Identification in psychotherapy. *International Journal of Psychotherapy, 6*, 109–116.

Westbrook, M. T., Legge, V., & Pennay, M. (1993). Attitudes towards disabilities in a multicultural society. *Social Science Medicine, 36*, 615–623.

White, K. P. (2002). Surviving hating and being hated. *Contemporary Psychoanalysis, 38*, 401– 422.

Word, C. O., Zanna, M. P., & Cooper, J. (1974). The nonverbal mediation of self-fulfilling prophencies in interracial interaction. *Journal of Experimental Social Psychology, 10*, 109–120.

Young-Bruehl, E. (1996). *The anatomy of prejudices.* Cambridge, MA: Harvard University Press.

Young-Bruehl, E. (2007). A brief history of prejudice studies. In H. Parens, A. Mahfouz, S. Twemlow, & D. Scharff (Eds.). *The future of prejudice: Psychoanalysis and the prevention of prejudice* (pp. 219–236). Lanham, MD: Rowman & Littlefield.

Author Index

Subject Index

About the Author

Ron Aviram, Ph.D., is Instructor in Clinical Psychology (in Psychiatry) at Columbia University College of Physicians and Surgeons. He is Supervisor of Psychotherapy at New York Presbyterian Hospital and is a graduate of the William Alanson White Institute of Psychiatry, Psychoanalysis, and Psychology. Dr. Aviram has published articles about the effect of stigma on the diagnosis and treatment of psychiatric conditions. He has written about object relations theory of prejudice and the relevance of integrating concepts from psychoanalysis and social psychology. He has a private practice in New York City.